0%

Tax-Free

*R*etirement

0%

Tax-Free

*R*etirement

Mark P. Haye

ISBN: 978-1-961650-01-5 (eBook)

ISBN: 978-1-961650-00-8 (Paperback)

Printed in the United States of America.

Published in the United States by GeeMorgan Publishing LLC

First printing edition 2023.

All inquiries about this book can be sent to the author at

markhaye@geemorganpublishing.com

or hello@geemorganpublishing.com

For more information, or to book an event, visit the website:
www.markhaye.com

GeeMorgan Publishing LLC

19046 Bruce B Downs Blvd #1016,

Tampa, FL 33647

www.geemorganpublishing.com

Dedication

For those embarking on the journey to a secure retirement, this book is your beacon. May it illuminate your path towards financial stability and peace in your golden years!

~MPH~

CONTENTS

Acknowledgment

In the journey of life, a few special souls have touched mine, carving an indelible mark, a precious legacy that I carry in my heart.

I am profoundly grateful for my father, Paul, and my stepmother, Ruth, for being my guiding stars, instilling in me a resilient spirit. To my mother, Rebecca, and stepdad, John, your love has been my sanctuary, your wisdom, my compass. To my brother Tim, his wife Tara, and their son Isaac, your unwavering support anchors me. My twin sister, Jennifer, her husband Ryan, and their lovely daughter, Elise, you are my mirror, my shadow, my joy. To the young, vibrant soul, Mason, having you in my life has brought a unique perspective. This nine-year-old boy, whom I care for deeply, demonstrates the will to live life to the fullest every day, reminding me that every moment is precious and should be treasured. Donnie, my best friend, your companionship fuels my spirit, while Charles, my business partner, your camaraderie invigorates my professional journey. My colleague Danny, your insights are invaluable, as are those of my exceptional staff - John, Rosa, and Jackie, who make work a pleasure. Lastly, to my clients, you inspire me, challenge me, and make all the hard work worthwhile.

This acknowledgment is but a small token of my immense gratitude to you all. Thank you.

Introduction

"If we command our wealth, we shall be rich and free. If our wealth commands us, we are poor indeed." —Edmund Burke, Economist

As the author of "0% Tax-Free Retirement," I've seen firsthand the importance of having a well-thought-out strategy for saving for retirement in today's fast-paced world. Unfortunately, many individuals are not prepared for their senior years due to a lack of financial literacy and retirement planning. Having worked in the banking sector for several years, I know that many people struggle when it comes to setting aside money for retirement.

Since earning my Master of Business Administration with a concentration in finance, I have made it my professional goal to assist clients in developing customized financial strategies that take full advantage of tax laws. Due to my extensive background, I have been honored as a member of the Million Dollar Round Table, the Court of the Table, and Top of the Table - MDRT, a distinction held by just 75 advisors globally.

For those who wish to plan ahead financially, 0% Tax-Free Retirement is an accessible educational manual. This book delves into the significance of knowing one's tax regulations and how to use them to one's advantage to generate several sources of income in retirement. We will help you plan for your retirement by examining the many options available to you in the marketplace, including permanent life insurance.

As we embark on a journey through this book, you'll gain a deeper comprehension of supplemental life insurance plans - this will be referred to throughout this book as LIRP/SLIRP (utilizing IRS code 7702) role in a comprehensive financial strategy, the challenges, and rewards of establishing multiple income streams during retirement, and the complexities of today's tax landscape. Discover how to transform taxable assets into tax-free retirement income and familiarize yourself with the regulations governing qualified and non-qualified funds.

The 0% Tax-Free Retirement is designed for individuals of all ages seeking to enhance their understanding of the economy and leverage tax laws to their benefit in retirement. Whether you're just launching your career or standing on the brink of retirement, this book offers valuable insights and concepts to secure your financial future.

Let's embark on the path to prosperity together, shaping a retirement plan that harnesses the power of applicable tax laws and instills the confidence that comes from being financially prepared for whatever the future holds.

Disclaimer

The advice in "0% Tax-Free Retirement" is based on my many years of practice as a financial counselor. However, the information included in this book is not meant to serve as personalized financial advice for any reader. The appropriate course of action for your own financial circumstances should be determined after consulting with a certified financial counselor or tax specialist.

Although this book covers a wide range of financial concepts and techniques, it is ultimately up to the reader to choose which ones are most applicable to their own situations. The author and publisher disclaim all liability for any injury that may arise from following the advice given in this book.

Finally, it is important to remember that the author's achievements in the subject may not always translate into financial success for the reader. Each person's financial circumstance is unique, making decision-making a very personal and intricate process. Never make a major financial move without first consulting a financial counselor and a tax expert.

Chapter 1

UNDERSTANDING TAX CODES

"Money grows on the tree of persistence." —Japanese proverb

As a well-certified financial advisor who has won multiple awards in my career, I believe that understanding the tax codes is a crucial aspect of retirement planning. Retirees can minimize their tax liabilities and maximize their retirement income by having a solid grasp of the various tax laws, guidelines, and regulations that govern how taxes are calculated and collected. Knowledge of the standard deduction can be especially useful in creating tax-free income during retirement.

One essential component of the tax code is the standard deduction. Income tax exemptions, or standard deductions, change depending on a person's age, filing status, and based on specific criteria. In 2023, for example, a married couple filing jointly will have a standard deduction of $27,700. Understanding how to satisfy the standard deduction using taxable assets can help create tax-free income during retirement.

One of my favorite strategies for meeting the standard deduction is to use qualified monies like IRA, 401k, 457, simple IRAs, 403b, SEP IRA, Solo 401(k), Thrift Savings Plan (TSP), 401(a) Plan, Defined Benefit Plan, Keogh Plan, ESOP, and Profit-Sharing Plan. These types of accounts provide tax deductions when contributions are made, but withdrawals are subject to income tax. Retirees can create tax-free income from their qualified monies by taking only the amount necessary to meet the standard deduction.

Another strategy is to use supplemental life insurance policies (SLIRP). These policies provide a tax-free death benefit, and the cash value can be used to generate tax-free income during retirement. Retirees can use the cash value to take loans and withdrawals without paying income tax.

Understanding tax codes also involves being aware of long-term care planning, as this can be a significant expense during retirement. Long-term care insurance premiums can be deductible if they exceed a certain threshold based on age and adjusted gross income. Additionally, retirees can use LIRP/SLIRP (7702) policies with long-term care riders to provide tax-free funds in the event of a long-term care need.

Explanation Of The Standard Deductions

What is Standard Deduction?

The standard deduction is a crucial part of your income that is exempt from taxation, and it can significantly lower your taxable income. Instead of using Schedule A of Form 1040 to itemize your deductions, the Internal Revenue Service (IRS) allows you to use the standard deduction. However, the amount of the deduction you can claim depends on various factors, such as your filing status, age, and whether you are claimed as a dependent on someone else's tax return. By understanding the standard deduction and how it applies to your specific situation, you can take advantage of all available deductions and keep more of your hard-earned money in your pocket. "0% Tax-Free Retirement" is an essential guide to understanding the standard deduction and other tax advantages to help you maximize your retirement income and minimize your tax burden.

How does it work?

A person's income is subject to a tax known as income tax, which is collected by the federal government and state governments. Remember that your annual earnings and your taxable income are two different things. This is because tax liability may be minimized by using deductions and credits provided by the government. Income that is subject to taxation is often less than total income because of various deductions.

Taxpayers have the option of taking either the standard deduction or a set of itemized deductions, both of which are recognized by the Internal Revenue Service. You may reduce your taxable income by an established amount known as the standard deduction, which is established by the government. On your yearly tax return, you may deduct this sum to lower your taxable income. Your tax filing status and the rate of inflation together determine your standard deduction.

A higher standard deduction is available to those who are 65 or older before the end of the tax year (the day before an individual's 65th birthday is the day they are considered to be 65). In 2022, the standard deduction for a person who is claimed as a dependent on someone else's tax return was the greater of $1,150 or the person's earned income + $400 (up to the amount of the basic standard deduction for the person's filing status).

In 2023, the standard deduction for a dependent will increase to $1,250, or the greater of the earned income and $400.

How To Take A Taxable Asset And Satisfy The Standard Deduction Only Making It Now Tax-Free.

To understand how to take a taxable asset and satisfy the standard deduction only making it tax-free now, it's essential to know that traditional IRAs, 401ks, 457s, 403bs, and other qualified retirement accounts are funded with pre-tax dollars. This means that when you contribute to these accounts, you get a tax deduction for that contribution in the year you make it, which lowers your taxable income for that year.

However, retirement withdrawals are taxed similarly to other sources of income. So, if you withdraw $50,000 from your traditional IRA during retirement, that $50,000 will be added to your taxable income for that year, and you will owe taxes on it at your marginal tax rate.

To make qualified monies tax-free during retirement, you can use these assets to satisfy the standard deduction. The standard deduction can be thought of as a tax-free buffer that you can use to shield a portion of your retirement income from taxes. For example, if the standard deduction for a married couple filing jointly is $27,700 in 2023, and you have $27,700 in taxable income during retirement, you could use your IRA to satisfy the standard deduction and make that $27,700 tax-free.

Taking into account your RMD for the year can help you withdraw the appropriate amount from your IRA to meet the standard deduction and avoid taxes. After reaching a specific age (usually 73 or 70 ½, depending on your birth date), the IRS mandates that you begin taking distributions from your traditional IRA and other eligible retirement accounts in accordance with the Required Minimum Distribution (RMD).

Imagine that you have determined that your RMD for the year is $30,000. As of right now, the $27,700 standard deduction applies to your filing situation. You may take out up to $27,700 tax-free from your IRA to cover your standard deduction. Since this amount is below the standard deduction threshold, it will not be subject to taxation.

The remaining $2,300 ($30,000 minus $27,700) of your RMD would be liable to income tax in this scenario. Taking out the amount necessary to cover the standard deduction, however, turns that sum into tax-free money.

The basic idea is to manage your IRA withdrawals in such a way that you take full benefit of the standard deduction and pay the least amount of tax possible. This method of withdrawing funds may help you pay less in taxes after you reach retirement age.

Once you know your RMD, you can subtract the standard deduction from that amount to determine how much you need to withdraw to satisfy the standard deduction. For example, if your RMD is $50,000, and the standard deduction is $27,700, you would need to withdraw $27,700 from your IRA to satisfy the standard deduction.

By using your IRA to satisfy the standard deduction, you can create tax-free income during retirement. You should consult a financial advisor or tax professional to determine how best to allocate your taxable retirement income to minimize your tax bill.

In this way, by utilizing qualified monies, one can create a stream of tax-free income during retirement. It is important to note that required minimum distributions (RMDs) must be taken from traditional retirement accounts starting at age 73, which can impact the amount of tax-free income that can be generated from these accounts.

See the Chart below for a visual representation RMD Factors:

New Uniform Lifetime Table

Age	Uniform Table RMD Factor	RMD as a % of Account Balance	Age	Uniform Table RMD Factor	RMD as a % of Account Balance
70	29.1	3.44%	96	8.3	12.05%
71	28.2	3.55%	97	7.8	12.83%
72	27.3	3.67%	98	7.3	13.70%
73	26.4	3.79%	99	6.8	14.71%
74	25.5	3.93%	100	6.4	15.63%
75	24.6	4.07%	101	5.9	16.95%
76	23.7	4.22%	102	5.6	17.86%
77	22.8	4.39%	103	5.2	19.24%
78	21.9	4.57%	104	4.9	20.41%
79	21	4.77%	105	4.6	21.74%
80	20.2	4.96%	106	4.3	23.26%
81	19.3	5.19%	107	4.1	24.40%
82	18.4	5.44%	108	3.9	25.65%
83	17.6	5.69%	109	3.7	27.03%
84	16.8	5.96%	110	3.5	28.58%
85	16	6.25%	111	3.4	29.42%
86	15.2	6.58%	112	3.2	31.25%
87	14.4	6.95%	113	3.1	32.26%
88	13.6	7.36%	114	3	33.34%
89	12.9	7.76%	115	2.9	34.49%
90	12.1	8.27%	116	2.8	35.72%
91	11.4	8.78%	117	2.7	37.04%
92	10.8	9.26%	118	2.5	40.00%
93	10.1	9.91%	119	2.3	43.48%
94	9.5	10.53%	120+	2	50.00%
95	8.9	11.24%			

Source: Internal Revenue Service, Updated Life Expectancy and Distribution Period Tables Used for Purposes of Determining Minimum Required Distributions. November 8, 2019

How Permanent Life Insurance Will Complement Standard Deductions And Generate Tax-Free Retirement Income.

You may save for retirement and meet the criteria of the standard deductions with permanent life insurance, such as whole life or indexed universal life. The idea is to augment retirement income with the cash value of the policy while simultaneously giving a death benefit to beneficiaries who have been designated by the policyholder.

Here's how it works: when you pay premiums for a permanent life insurance policy, a portion of that payment goes toward the policy's death benefit. The cash value grows over time, often in a tax-deferred manner, and policyholders have the option of taking cash out of their policies or taking out loans against their policies.

Policy loans and withdrawals from a permanent life insurance policy can be taken up to any amount, completely tax-free. These funds are not subject to income tax and will remain untaxed when received during retirement.

The cash value of a permanent life insurance policy not only helps you meet the criteria for a tax-free retirement but can also be used to supplement your income during those golden years, without any tax implications. By leveraging this tax-free income stream, you can effectively complement your retirement income from other sources, such as Social Security or pensions. Policyholders can make withdrawals from or borrow against their policies, providing additional financial flexibility in retirement.

It is essential to be aware that making withdrawals or taking out policy loans from a permanent life insurance policy might affect the death benefit of the policy as well as the capacity of the policyholder to pay future premiums. When utilizing permanent life insurance as a strategy for retirement income, careful thought and attention should be given to each aspect of the policy.

A LIRP/SLIRP (Life Insurance Retirement Plan/Supplemental Life Insurance Retirement Plan) serves as a valuable source of tax-free income during your retirement years. Not only does it provide tax-free funds while you're alive, but it also offers tax-free benefits in case you don't reach retirement or need long-term care.

One essential aspect of retirement planning is the waiver of premiums feature. If you become disabled, this feature ensures that the life insurance company will continue funding your LIRP/SLIRP plan on your behalf. Unlike a traditional 401k plan, which might not receive contributions in the event of your disability, the waiver of premiums guarantees that your LIRP/SLIRP remains funded, securing your financial future.

In summary, a LIRP/SLIRP offers a comprehensive approach to retirement planning, providing tax-free income, long-term care benefits, and financial security in the event of disability through the waiver of premiums feature. This plan ensures peace of mind and a stable financial future during your retirement years.

Life Insurance Retirement Plan (LIRP) offers a death benefit in addition to a cash value-building component. This sort of policy is meant to stay in effect for the whole of the policy's term. In contrast to traditional retirement plans like 401(k)s and IRAs, a LIRP/SLIRP has the potential to provide retirees with income that is not subject to taxes.

A LIRP's cash value may build up tax-deferred growth and gives its owners tax-free access to that growth via withdrawals and policy loans. This growth is accumulated over time. This might provide a source of retirement income exempt from taxes and does not need to comply with required minimum distributions (RMDs) the way traditional retirement plans do. To put it another way, you won't need to worry about your finances being depleted.

An income from a LIRP/SLIRP is excluded from taxes if you become incapacitated or need long-term care. Suppose the policyholder suffers from a disability that prevents them from working. In that case, the insurance company may agree to waive the policyholder's premium payments so that the policy may continue to mature and provide income that is exempt from taxes in the future.

This may be of particular relevance when it comes to planning for retirement since it may provide a source of income that is exempt from taxation after retirement regardless of the occurrence of unanticipated events such as the need for long-term care or a disability. This may be of particular value when it comes to preparing for retirement. Individuals who utilize LIRP as a tool for planning their retirement can produce a tax-free income stream unaffected by the stock market and other factors that may be found in the wider world.

It is crucial to stress that a LIRP or any other kind of permanent life insurance is not meant to replace traditional retirement plans like a 401(k), an individual retirement account (IRA), or a Roth IRA. This is because these traditional retirement plans are designed to help individuals save money for their retirement. You should see it more as a supplemental tool that might potentially increase your income after retirement and provide extra tax benefits.

It is crucial to carefully evaluate the costs and fees associated with LIRP (Life Insurance Retirement Plan) plans. With a typical LIRP plan, you might pay a 1% fee for the life of the contract, which could span 30-40 years. It's essential to understand the benefits you receive in exchange for that 1% fee. These benefits include tax-free income, death benefits, long-term care, and advantageous tax code provisions. On the other hand, a traditional 401k plan does not offer these benefits.

Before committing to a LIRP, it is highly recommended to consult with a knowledgeable and experienced financial advisor who specializes in LIRP and other permanent life insurance policies for retirement planning. This guidance is necessary because determining the exact amount of money you will need for retirement can be a complex task. A qualified financial consultant can help you make the best decision for your specific financial goals and retirement needs.

The Benefits Of Using Permanent Life Insurance For Retirement Planning

Permanent life insurance can offer several benefits when used for retirement planning. Some of these benefits include:

1. **Tax-free income:** A retirement income not subject to taxation is one of the primary advantages of having permanent life insurance. This indicates that you can receive a stream of income exempt from income taxes, which may help you reduce the amount of money you spend on taxes and boost the amount of money you have coming in during your retirement years.
2. **Death benefit protection:** Permanent life insurance plans often include a death benefit that, in the case of the policyholder's death, may serve as a source of financial security for the surviving family members and loved ones. It's important to remember this if you support a family that depends on your salary, whether it's young children or old parents.
3. **Cash value growth:** Another benefit of permanent life insurance is that it can build cash value over time, which can be used to supplement your retirement income. The cash value grows tax-deferred, which means that you do not have to pay taxes on the growth until you withdraw it. (Mark R Moore)
4. **Long-Term Care Provision:** One often-overlooked benefit of permanent life insurance is its potential utility in covering long-term care expenses. If a long-term care event arises, you can leverage the death benefit while you're still alive to help cover the costs associated with such care. This can be a critical tool in protecting your retirement savings from the high costs of long-term care services, which can quickly deplete your nest egg. Remember to consult with a financial advisor to ensure this strategy aligns with your overall retirement plan and personal circumstances.

5. **Flexible access to funds:** With LIRP policies, you can access the cash value in the policy tax-free through loans and withdrawals. This can provide you with greater flexibility in managing your retirement income and can help you avoid penalties for early withdrawals from traditional retirement accounts.
6. **Protection against market volatility:** Because permanent life insurance plans give a minimum interest rate that is guaranteed, these policies might offer some amount of protection against the volatility of the market. This may be of utmost significance for those who are getting close to retirement or who have a poor tolerance for risk.
7. **Estate planning benefits:** Permanent life insurance plans may also provide advantages for estate planning, such as leaving money to your heirs without paying taxes on the transfer of capital. This may assist you in guaranteeing that your assets are divided according to your preferences and leave a legacy for the people you care about when you pass away.

Overall, permanent life insurance can be a powerful tool for retirement planning, offering tax-free income, death benefit protection, cash value growth, flexible access to funds, protection against market volatility, and estate planning benefits. The prices and expenses of these products should be carefully considered, and a financial adviser should be consulted to assist you in deciding whether they are appropriate for your situation and long-term objectives.

The Largest Tax Break In The IRS Code And Long-Term Care Planning May Destroy Any Retirement Plan.

The tax-deferred growth of retirement funds such as conventional IRAs, 401(k)s, 403(b)s, and accounts that are very similar to these types of accounts is the greatest tax benefit in our tax law. This implies that the contributions you make to these accounts will not be subject to taxation in the year in which they are made; rather, the taxes will be postponed until the time when you withdraw the assets after retirement. Your assets will be able to compound over time thanks to the tax-deferred growth, which may result in a sizeable amount of money for your retirement.

On the other hand, the costs of long-term care may swiftly drain retirement funds and reverse all of the advantages of growth that have been tax-deferred. Long-term care is the spectrum of medical and personal support required by those who are no longer able to care for themselves independently as a result of chronic disease, accident, or disability. Long-term care is referred to as "long-term assistance" or "long-term care." Long-term care may come with a very hefty price tag, yet the majority of health insurance plans and Medicare do not cover the expense.

It is possible to protect oneself against this danger by including permanent life insurance coverage in one's retirement planning approach. To be more specific, a life insurance retirement plan (LIRP) may provide a stream of income that is exempt from taxes during retirement, which can then be used to pay for the costs of long-term care. This is because the cash value of a LIRP may be withdrawn without incurring any taxes and can be used for any use, including paying for long-term care costs.

The ability to defer premium payments is a crucial part of a long-term care insurance plan (LIRP). The policy's waiver of premium clause will allow it to remain in force even if premium payments are waived if you become incapacitated and are unable to work. Therefore, if you become disabled or unwell, your retirement funds, which are held in the form of a LIRP, would not be negatively impacted.

In conclusion, while having the development of retirement savings exempt from taxation is a big tax benefit, it is essential to also prepare for the possibility of having to pay for long-term care services. A LIRP may be used to pay for long-term care needs and can give tax-free income during retirement. Additionally, the waiver of the premium provision can guarantee that the policy continues to be in effect even in the case of a disability or sickness.

Personal Work Sheet

Tax Efficiency Analysis

Taxed Currently		Taxed Later		Taxed Never*	
Checking/Savings	$______	IRAs, SEP IRAs	$______	Roth IRAs/401 (k)	$______
CDs	$______	SIMPLE IRAs 401 (k), 403 (B)	$______	Municipal Bonds	$______
Stock Mutual Funds	$______			Universal Life Insurance	$______
Bond Mutual Funds	$______	Pension Plans	$______	Whole Life Insurance	$______
Stocks	$______	Variable Annuities	$______		
Bonds	$______	Fixed Annuities	$______	529 College Plans	$______
UGMA	$______	Savings Bonds	$______	Coverdale Education IRA	$______
Other	$______	Other	$______	Other	$______
Current Total	$______	Current Total	$______	Current Total	$______
	______%		______%		______%

Are Your Investments Increasing or Decreasing Your Tax Burden?

1. Tax Deductible? 2. Tax Deferred? 3. Tax Free?	*Certain Events and distributions may be subject to taxation and individuals would be responsible for the appropriate liability. 1099s may be required for informational purposes only, under certain circumstances. This piece provides general information regarding the Internal Revenue Code and does not take into consideration specific state laws.

Haye P. (2015)

Chapter 2

MEETING THE STANDARD DEDUCTIONS WITH TAXABLE MONIES

(Qualified Monies)

Meeting the standard deductions with taxable monies refers to a strategy of using qualified monies, such as traditional IRA, 401(k), 403(b), or 457 plans, to offset taxable income and reduce or eliminate taxes owed. A person's taxable income may be reduced by making use of the standard deduction, which varies according to their filing status, age, and based on specific criteria. It is a deduction that reduces the amount of income that is subject to tax.

When a taxpayer has taxable income, they may have to pay taxes on that income at their current tax rate. However, by using qualified monies, they can reduce their taxable income and potentially lower their tax rate. For example, if a taxpayer has $50,000 in taxable income and invested $10,000 in qualified monies, they can use the $10,000 to reduce their taxable income to $40,000, which may put them in a lower tax bracket and reduce their tax liability.

To take advantage of this strategy, the taxpayer must withdraw the qualified monies from their account, pay any applicable taxes on the distribution, and then use the remaining funds to cover their living expenses. This process must be done strategically to avoid triggering additional taxes or penalties, such as the early withdrawal penalty for those under the age of 59 ½.

It is important to note that while this strategy can be effective in reducing or eliminating taxes, it may not be suitable for everyone. It is imperative that you have a conversation with a financial counselor or tax specialist to establish whether or not this plan is suitable for your specific personal circumstances and monetary objectives.

Explanation Of How Your IRA Can Be Used To Meet The Standard Deductions.

Your IRA (Individual Retirement Account) can be used to meet the standard deductions by strategically withdrawing funds from your IRA to cover your living expenses, thereby reducing your taxable income and potentially lowering your tax liability. Here's how it works in more detail:

Traditional IRA

If you have a standard individual retirement account (IRA), any contributions that you make to the account are normally deductible in the same year that they are made, and any profits that accumulate in the account are not subject to taxation until the individual decides to take them out of the account. When you reach the age of 59 and a half, you are eligible to begin drawing distributions from your standard individual retirement account (IRA) without being subject to the tax penalty for early withdrawal. Withdrawals made from a conventional IRA, on the other hand, are treated as taxable income and subject to taxation at the same rates as regular income.

To meet the standard deductions using your traditional IRA, you can strategically withdraw funds from your IRA in an amount that keeps your taxable income below the standard deduction threshold. For example, if the standard deduction for a married couple filing jointly is $27,700 (for the tax year 2023), you can withdraw that amount from your traditional IRA and use it to cover your living expenses. This would effectively reduce your taxable income to zero, resulting in no taxes owed.

Roth IRA

Roth IRA contributions are made with after-tax dollars, meaning they are not tax-deductible in the year of contribution. However, the earnings on a Roth IRA grow tax-free, and qualified withdrawals from a Roth IRA are tax-free as well. This makes Roth IRA withdrawals a good option for meeting the standard deductions without incurring any taxes.

To meet the standard deductions using your Roth IRA, you can simply withdraw the necessary amount from your Roth IRA and use it to cover your living expenses. Since qualified withdrawals from a Roth IRA are tax-free, this will not result in any taxes owed and will effectively reduce your taxable income to zero.

It's important to note that IRA withdrawals are subject to certain rules and regulations, and not all withdrawals may be tax-free or penalty-free. For example, withdrawals from a traditional IRA before the age of 59 ½ may be subject to a 10% early withdrawal penalty, and Roth IRA withdrawals may have restrictions on the timing and types of withdrawals that are tax-free. If you want to be sure that your IRA use is in accordance with the relevant tax rules and regulations, you should talk to a financial counselor or tax specialist.

Hitting the Standard Deduction Sweet Spot: Utilizing RMDs with $500-650k in Qualified Monies

The statement "500 – 650k" of qualified monies is the sweet spot to hit the standard deduction using the required minimum distributions (RMD) scale" likely refers to a strategy that aims to maximize the benefits of qualified retirement accounts, such as traditional IRAs, 401(k)s, 403(b)s, and other similar retirement plans, concerning the standard deduction.

Here's a breakdown of the explanation:

Qualified Monies

Generally speaking, assets that are maintained in tax-advantaged retirement accounts, such as conventional IRAs, 401(k)s, 403(b)s, and other retirement plans that are functionally equivalent are referred to as qualified monies. Individuals can put money away for their retirement in a tax-deferred manner via the use of these accounts. This means that the contributions are made with already taxed money, and the profits are not subject to taxation until the account holder reaches retirement age.

Standard Deduction

Taxpayers can reduce their total tax obligation by using a deduction known as the standard deduction. This deduction is a predetermined amount that has been established by the Internal Revenue Service (IRS). The standard deduction is a tax break available to filers who do not want to itemize their deductions and is adjusted upward each year for inflation.

Required Minimum Distributions (RMDs):

According to the regulations set out by the IRS, required minimum distributions (RMDs) are the minimum sums that persons who have eligible retirement accounts are required to take from their accounts after they reach the age of 73 (or the age of 70 ½ for those who reached 70 ½ before January 1, 2020). RMDs are calculated according to the individual's life expectancy and the amount in their account, constituting taxable income.

Sweet Spot

It is probable that the phrase "sweet spot" relates to an ideal approach that attempts to withdraw just enough money from eligible retirement funds to meet the amount allowed for the standard deduction without exceeding the limit. This would lower the individual's taxable income, and as a consequence, the individual's tax due would be reduced.

500-650k Of Qualified Monies

The statement implies that taking required minimum distributions (RMDs) from eligible retirement funds in an amount ranging from $500,000 to $650,000 might correspond with the amount that can be deducted using the standard deduction. This would imply that the individual's taxable income would be decreased by the amount of the standard deduction; hence, the individual's prospective tax obligation would be lowered as well.

Depending on several variables, including one's situation, retirement planning, and tax preparation might be challenging. A knowledgeable financial expert or tax adviser should be consulted to get individualized counsel and assistance in ensuring that any proposed methods are suitable and in accordance with the most recent tax laws and regulations.

See Below For RMD Scale:

New Uniform Lifetime Table					
Age	Uniform Table RMD Factor	RMD as a % of Account Balance	Age	Uniform Table RMD Factor	RMD as a % of Account Balance
70	29.1	3.44%	96	8.3	12.05%
71	28.2	3.55%	97	7.8	12.83%
72	27.3	3.67%	98	7.3	13.70%
73	26.4	3.79%	99	6.8	14.71%
74	25.5	3.93%	100	6.4	15.63%
75	24.6	4.07%	101	5.9	16.95%
76	23.7	4.22%	102	5.6	17.86%
77	22.8	4.39%	103	5.2	19.24%
78	21.9	4.57%	104	4.9	20.41%
79	21	4.77%	105	4.6	21.74%
80	20.2	4.96%	106	4.3	23.26%
81	19.3	5.19%	107	4.1	24.40%
82	18.4	5.44%	108	3.9	25.65%
83	17.6	5.69%	109	3.7	27.03%
84	16.8	5.96%	110	3.5	28.58%
85	16	6.25%	111	3.4	29.42%
86	15.2	6.58%	112	3.2	31.25%
87	14.4	6.95%	113	3.1	32.26%
88	13.6	7.36%	114	3	33.34%
89	12.9	7.76%	115	2.9	34.49%
90	12.1	8.27%	116	2.8	35.72%
91	11.4	8.78%	117	2.7	37.04%
92	10.8	9.26%	118	2.5	40.00%
93	10.1	9.91%	119	2.3	43.48%
94	9.5	10.53%	120+	2	50.00%
95	8.9	11.24%			

Source: Internal Revenue Service, Updated Life Expectancy and Distribution Period Tables Used for Purposes of Determining Minimum Required Distributions. November 8, 2019

Calculating The Amount Of IRA Monies Needed To Meet The Standard Deductions

To calculate the amount of IRA monies needed to meet the standard deductions, we need to determine the current year's standard deduction for the taxpayer. As of 2023, the standard deduction for a married couple filing jointly is $27,700.

Assuming that the married couple only has taxable income from their IRA and wants to use it to meet the standard deduction, we can calculate the required amount by dividing the standard deduction by the effective tax rate. An individual's effective tax rate is the rate at which each dollar of taxable income is actually taxed.

> ***For instance, let's consider a married couple who has $500,000 in qualified funds. If they decide to withdraw 5% of this amount, they will receive $25,000 as income. In this scenario, the first $25,000 withdrawn is tax-free, allowing the couple to enjoy their income without any tax burden.***

Regarding the tipping point of $500k, this refers to the point at which the required minimum distributions (RMDs) become a significant factor in retirement planning. Once an IRA owner reaches age 73, they are required by law to begin taking required minimum distributions (RMDs). The amount is calculated based on the account balance and life expectancy.

For example, if the account balance is $500,000 and the account holder's life expectancy is 25 years, the RMD would be approximately $18,518.52 ($500,000/25). As the account balance increases, so does the RMD, which can lead to higher taxes and potentially push the taxpayer into a higher tax bracket.

In summary, the amount of IRA monies needed to meet the standard deduction can be calculated by dividing the standard deduction by the effective tax rate. The tipping point of $500k refers to the point at which RMDs become a significant factor in retirement planning.

The Tax Benefits Of Using Qualified Monies To Meet The Standard Deductions.

Using qualified monies, such as traditional IRA or 401(k) accounts, to meet the standard deductions can provide several tax benefits. These include:

1. Tax Deduction: Contributions made to traditional IRA or 401(k) accounts are typically tax-deductible in the year of contribution. This means that the amount contributed reduces the taxpayer's taxable income for that year, potentially lowering their overall tax liability. For example, if a taxpayer contributes $5,000 to a traditional IRA and falls in the 22% tax bracket, their taxable income would be reduced by $5,000, resulting in a tax savings of $1,100 (22% of $5,000).

2. Tax-Deferred Growth: Qualified monies in traditional IRA or 401(k) accounts grow on a tax-deferred basis, which means that the investment earnings are not subject to current income taxes. This allows the investments to potentially grow faster over time, as the taxpayer can reinvest the earnings that would have otherwise been paid in taxes.

3. Lower Tax Bracket in Retirement: Using qualifying funds to fulfill the standard deductions might be beneficial if the person anticipates being in a lower tax band after retirement than during their working years. This is because the withdrawals from traditional IRA or 401(k) accounts during retirement are subject to ordinary income tax. If the taxpayer's income is lower in retirement, they may pay a lower tax rate on the withdrawals, resulting in overall tax savings.

4. Flexibility in Timing of Taxable Income: Traditional IRA or 401(k) withdrawals are generally subject to required minimum distributions (RMDs) starting at age 73. This means that the taxpayer has some flexibility in timing their taxable income during retirement. By

carefully managing their withdrawals, they can control their taxable income each year and potentially stay within lower tax brackets, optimizing their tax situation.

5. Estate Planning Benefits: Using qualified monies to meet the standard deductions can also provide estate planning benefits. Upon the death of the account holder, qualified monies can be passed on to beneficiaries with potential tax advantages, such as the ability to stretch out the distributions over the beneficiaries' lifetime, potentially reducing the overall tax impact.

The tax advantages of employing eligible funds to fulfill the standard deductions may vary based on an individual's situation and the current tax rules and regulations. If you need specialized advice, it's advisable to see a tax professional or financial advisor.

Creating Taxable Income Into Tax-Free Income.

There are a variety of financial techniques and vehicles that, when used properly, may assist in lowering or even eliminating the need to pay taxes on investment income. Utilizing a Roth Individual Retirement Account (IRA) is one such technique.

A Roth IRA is a specific kind of individual retirement account (IRA) that enables contributions to be made after taxes have already been paid. This means that contributions to a Roth IRA do not qualify for a tax deduction in the year they are made. However, any profits that are generated from the contributions are not subject to taxation, and any withdrawals that meet the criteria for a Roth IRA are similarly not subject to taxation. This signifies that the investment income created inside a Roth IRA has the potential to be tax-free when it is taken during retirement since Roth IRAs are not subject to federal income tax.

Since a Roth IRA is funded using after-tax dollars, the contributor does not get an immediate tax break like they would with a traditional IRA or 401(k). The potential tax-free status of withdrawals from a Roth

IRA in retirement, on the other hand, makes it a potentially attractive option for long-term tax planning.

When investors put money into a Roth individual retirement account (IRA), they position themselves to take advantage of the tax-free status of both their contributions and their profits at retirement, assuming that they meet the criteria for tax-free withdrawals. This may be particularly beneficial for persons who anticipate being in a higher tax band during retirement since it enables them to possibly avoid paying taxes on the increase of their assets. This is especially favorable for those who expect to be at a higher tax rate during retirement.

It is essential to be aware that contributions to Roth IRAs are restricted by income caps and that there are additional laws and constraints around withdrawals, distributions, and other actions involving Roth IRAs. Remember that tax laws and regulations are subject to change at any moment and that everyone's financial position is different. Therefore, it is highly encouraged to speak with a skilled tax expert or financial counselor to assess whether or not a Roth IRA or other options for tax planning are suitable for your particular circumstance.

Personal Work Sheet

Tax Efficiency Analysis

Taxed Currently		Taxed Later		Taxed Never*	
Checking/Savings	$__________	IRAs, SEP IRAs	$__________	Roth IRAs/401 (k)	$__________
CDs	$__________	SIMPLE IRAs 401 (k), 403 (B)	$__________	Municipal Bonds	$__________
Stock Mutual Funds	$__________			Universal Life Insurance	$__________
Bond Mutual Funds	$__________	Pension Plans	$__________	Whole Life Insurance	$__________
Stocks	$__________	Variable Annuities	$__________		
Bonds	$__________	Fixed Annuities	$__________	529 College Plans	$__________
UGMA	$__________	Savings Bonds	$__________	Coverdale Education IRA	$__________
Other	$__________	Other	$__________	Other	$__________
Current Total	$__________	Current Total	$__________	Current Total	$__________
	__________%		__________%		__________%

Are Your Investments Increasing or Decreasing Your Tax Burden?

1. Tax Deductible?
2. Tax Deferred?
3. Tax Free?

*Certain Events and distributions may be subject to taxation and individuals would be responsible for the appropriate liability. 1099s may be required for informational purposes only, under certain circumstances. This piece provides general information regarding the Internal Revenue Code and does not take into consideration specific state laws.

Haye P. (2015)

Chapter 3

WHAT ARE ROTH 401K AND ROTH IRA, AND HOW DO THEY DIFFER FROM TRADITIONAL 401KS AND IRAS?

Contributions to a Roth 401(k) or Roth IRA are not tax deductible in the year they are made, but you may be eligible for a tax refund when you remove the funds. The returns on these contributions, however, grow tax-free, and withdrawals from Roth accounts that meet certain criteria are similarly tax-free. Let's go at the specifics of each of these:

1. Roth 401(k): The Roth 401(k) as "a popular employee benefit option that is similar to the traditional 401(k) in many ways." Both programs provide opportunities for workers to set aside a percentage of their pay towards retirement. However, unlike standard 401(k) contributions, which are made with pre-tax monies, Roth 401(k) contributions are made using after-tax earnings (Investopedia, 2023).

The maximum amount you may put into a Roth 401(k) in 2023 is $22,500 (Investopedia, 2023); if you're 50 or older, you can put in an extra $7,500. Employee and employer contributions are capped at the lesser of $66,000 or 100% of base salary. For those over the age of 50, the maximum annual contribution is $67,500 (Investopedia, 2023), with an additional $7,500 in "catch-up" contributions.

Earnings on Roth 401(k) contributions increase tax-free, and so do withdrawals from the account, provided they meet certain criteria.

This implies that in retirement, you may be able to take your Roth 401(k)'s investment earnings tax-free. Moreover, unlike a Roth IRA, a Roth 401(k) does not place any restrictions on the amount of money a person may put into their account each year based on their income level (Investopedia, 2023).

Annual contribution limits for a Roth 401(k) are set by the Internal Revenue Service (IRS), and there are laws and restrictions governing withdrawals. Roth 401(k) contributions are subject to the regulations and restrictions of the contributing employer. To learn more about your company's Roth 401(k) plan, you should read the plan paperwork and talk to a financial counsellor.

2. Roth IRA: Some individuals opt to invest their after-tax income in a Roth IRA as a way to save for retirement. If you are eligible, your contributions to a Roth IRA are not tax deductible, but withdrawals and earnings from the account are. The Roth IRA contribution maximum for people under the age of 50 is $6,500, while those 50 and beyond may put away $7,500 (Fidelity, 2023).

The freedom from restrictions that comes with a Roth IRA is a major perk. Contributions to a Roth IRA are made after taxes have already been paid, and the account holder is not subject to RMDs (required minimum distributions) throughout their lifetime. This allows the Roth IRA to be utilized as a tax-efficient savings vehicle for long-term development, with the added benefit of tax-free withdrawals in retirement and no required minimum distributions (RMDs).

Individuals with higher incomes may not be able to make direct contributions to a Roth IRA due to income constraints. In 2023, you will not be able to make a Roth IRA contribution if your modified Adjusted Gross Income (AGI) is more than $228,000 and you are married filing jointly or an eligible widow(er).

For the year 2023, the following are the maximum contributions that may be made to a Roth 401(k) or Roth IRA:

There is a $22,500 cap on Roth 401(k) contributions each year. For those who are 50 or older, the catch-up contribution ceiling is $7,500, increasing the total allowed contribution amount to $30,000.

The maximum amount an employer may put into an employee's Roth 401(k) in a year is $66,000 or 100% of that person's salary, whichever is less. The maximum amount of contributions, including the catch-up contribution, that employees over the age of 50 may make is $67,500.

In 2023, persons under the age of 50 may put away a maximum of $6,500 into a Roth IRA, while those 50 and over can put away a maximum of $7,500. However, there are limits on how much you may put into a Roth IRA based on your annual income. If your modified adjusted gross income (AGI) is less than $138,000, you may contribute up to the maximum if you are single, head of household, or married filing separately (and did not reside with your spouse at any point during the year). A reduced amount may be contributed to a Roth IRA if your adjusted gross income is between $138,000 and $153,000, and no contributions can be made if your AGI is more than $153,000. If your combined annual income is less than $218,000, you may make a maximum contribution as a married couple or as an eligible widow(er). You can only make a partial contribution to a Roth IRA if your adjusted gross income is between $218,000 and $228,000, and you can't make any contributions at all if it's more than $228,000.

Roth Account Tax Advantages: Tax-Free Growth and Withdrawals in Retirement

Roth 401(k)s and Roth IRAs provide many tax benefits over ordinary 401(k)s and IRAs. The key perk is that withdrawals and gains aren't taxed after you reach retirement age. What happens is this:

To a Roth IRA, you may only contribute money that you have previously paid taxes on. Contributions themselves are taxable, but any subsequent increase is not. That implies your interest and capital gains from investments will be tax-free. Furthermore, there is no tax imposed on the withdrawals made after retirement.

Contributions to a conventional account reduce your taxable income in the year of contribution since they are made with pre-tax cash. Taxes on the earnings of your investments will be deferred until you withdraw the funds in retirement. ("When is a forex trade taxable? | Forex Academy") Withdrawing the funds, however, will result in taxable income and may raise your tax liability.

Although a Roth IRA doesn't provide an immediate tax reduction, it does allow for tax-free growth and withdrawals once retirement age is reached. This might be particularly helpful if you anticipate a higher effective tax rate in retirement than you do now. With a Roth IRA, you have greater control over your retirement income and tax liabilities since you are not subject to RMDs (required minimum distributions) throughout your lifetime.

It's important to remember that there are restrictions on how much of your income may be put into a Roth IRA, but no such restrictions on how much can be put into a Roth 401(k). To maximize your tax-free income in retirement, it may be wise to put money into both a Roth 401(k) and a Roth IRA if you can.

The Contribution Limits For Roth Accounts, And How They Compare To Traditional Accounts

The Internal Revenue Service (IRS) establishes the yearly contribution limitations for Roth accounts such as Roth 401(k)s and Roth IRAs. Contributions to a Roth IRA in 2023 are capped at $7,500 for individuals 50 and older and $6,500 for those under 50. These restrictions apply to the total amount that may be contributed to an individual's various IRA accounts.

The contribution maximum for Roth 401(k) accounts in 2023 is set at $19,500 for those who are younger than age 50 and $26,000 for those who are older than age 50. These restrictions apply to contributions made by the employee as well as those made by the employer. It is essential to be aware that certain firms cannot provide Roth 401(k)s as an option for their employees to invest in.

Roth accounts are similar to standard accounts in that they both have restrictions on the amount of money that may be contributed to the account each year. However, contributions to Roth accounts are made using money that has already been taxed, which means that taxes have been deducted from the total amount of the contribution before it is deposited into the account. Traditional accounts, on the other hand, are financed with money that was put away before taxes were taken out. This means that you will be responsible for paying taxes on the money when you take it out during retirement.

Keep in mind that high-income earners may not be eligible to make direct contributions to a Roth IRA or make contributions at all since income limits apply to Roth IRAs. This is something that should be kept in mind since it is crucial.

Considering Your Current and Future Tax Bracket: Roth vs. Traditional Account Contributions

You should think about your present tax rate and your expected tax bracket in retirement when picking between a Roth and a standard retirement plan.

Contributing to a conventional account may make sense if you are in a lower tax band now than you anticipate being in retirement. This is because of the tax benefits associated with making charitable contributions this year. Withdrawals made after retirement, however, will be subject to taxation at your rate at the time of withdrawal.

On the other side, a Roth IRA contribution may be preferable if your current tax band is greater than what you anticipate it would be in retirement. A primary tax benefit of a Roth IRA is that withdrawals in retirement are tax-free, even if contributions are made using after-tax cash, and don't reduce current taxable income.

Since tax regulations and your financial status are both subject to change, it might be difficult to estimate what tax band you will be in in the future. Therefore, it is wise to speak with a financial counselor about the sort of retirement plan that is most suited to your needs.

Benefits of Roth IRAs in Tax-Free Retirement Income

Because of its special tax benefits, the Roth IRA stands out among other retirement investing options. When funding a Roth IRA, you do it with money that has already been taxed. The real benefit of Roth IRAs, however, is their ability to grow tax-free. If you fulfill the requirements, your assets inside a Roth IRA may increase substantially over the course of many decades, and you won't have to pay taxes on any of that gain when you take the money in retirement.

Tax savings from a Roth IRA may be maximized by following the withdrawal regulations. To withdraw gains from a Roth IRA tax- and penalty-free, the account must have been open for at least five years, and the distribution must be made after the account holder turns 59½. There are situations when you may be allowed to withdraw cash early without incurring penalties, such as when you are a first-time homeowner or have very particular medical expenditures. Retirement income may be kept tax-free with careful planning and an understanding of these restrictions.

Roth IRA Conversion Strategy

To convert a conventional IRA to a Roth IRA is to make the corresponding transfer of assets. If you anticipate being in a higher tax bracket in retirement, this is a common method used to maximize the tax advantages of a Roth IRA.

The tax consequences are an important part of a Roth IRA conversion. Taxes must be paid on the after-tax contributions and profits that are converted from a regular IRA to a Roth IRA. You will only have to pay this tax once, and then, if you fulfill the requirements, your retirement savings may grow tax-free and be taken tax-free when you reach retirement age.

Consider both the short-term tax implications and the possible long-term rewards. Paying taxes now at a lower rate might be beneficial if you anticipate a higher tax rate in retirement. You have greater control over your retirement income with a Roth IRA since there are no RMDs during your lifetime, and the tax advantages may be passed on to your descendants.

Retirement planning should take into account both the Roth IRA, with its tax-free growth, and the Roth IRA Conversion, with its strategic long-term tax benefits. Which one is best for you will depend on your current and future income, tax bracket, and retirement objectives. The only way to make it through these choices is to consult with a financial expert who can provide you with individualized recommendations.

Potential Limitations of Roth Accounts: Income Limits, Contributions, and Early Withdrawal Penalties

While Roth accounts offer many tax advantages, they do come with some potential limitations. Here are some examples:

Income Limits For Contributions

Unlike traditional accounts, Roth accounts have income limits for contributions. In 2023, if your modified adjusted gross income (MAGI) exceeds $144,000 as a single filer or $214,000 as a married couple filing jointly, you cannot contribute to a Roth IRA. Similarly, if you earn too much as a high-income earner, you may not be able to contribute to a Roth 401(k) plan.

Early Withdrawal Penalties

Roth accounts are designed to encourage long-term retirement savings, and as such, there are penalties for early withdrawals. If you withdraw money from a Roth IRA or Roth 401(k) before age 59 1/2 and you haven't held the account for at least five years, you may be subject to a 10% penalty on the amount withdrawn. There are exceptions to this penalty, such as for certain medical expenses or first-time home purchases. (Jeff Rose CFP®, “7 Things You Need To Know About Simple IRAs (for 2023)

No Tax Deduction For Contributions

While Roth contributions grow tax-free and can be withdrawn tax-free in retirement, you don't receive a tax deduction for contributions as you do with traditional accounts. This means that if you are in a high tax bracket now and expect to be in a lower tax bracket in retirement, contributing to a traditional account may make more sense.

Investment Options May Be Limited

Roth accounts are still relatively new, and some employers may not offer a Roth 401(k) option. Additionally, the investment options available in Roth 401(k) plans may be more limited than those in traditional 401(k) plans. It's important to evaluate the investment options available in your employer's plan before deciding to contribute to a Roth account.

Liquidity Rules: Comparing Roth 401(k)s and Roth IRAs in Retirement Planning

The liquidity criteria for Roth 401(k) plans and Roth IRAs are not the same, which might have a variety of implications for your retirement planning.

A Roth 401(k) is a retirement plan that is sponsored by an employer, whereas a Roth IRA is a retirement plan that is sponsored by an individual. The distinction between the two is highlighted by the fact that required minimum distributions (RMDs) begin to be taken from a Roth 401(k) account at the age of 73, but a Roth individual retirement account (IRA) does not have RMDs throughout the original owner's lifetime.

In terms of the regulations governing liquidity, a Roth 401(k) has restricted possibilities for withdrawals before the age of 59 and one half, except for certain qualifying conditions such as a disability or severe financial difficulty. If you remove money from a Roth 401(k) before you become 59 and a half years old, in addition to having to pay taxes on the distribution, you may also be subject to a 10% early withdrawal penalty.

On the other hand, withdrawals from Roth IRAs are often subject to greater latitude than those from traditional IRAs. You can withdraw your contributions tax- and penalty-free at any time, and you are also able to withdraw your earnings tax- and penalty-free when you have reached the age of 59 and a half or if you satisfy certain qualifying circumstances such as being disabled or buying your first house.

In general, the liquidity limitations for Roth accounts may affect your retirement planning. This is particularly true if you believe you will need access to your money before you become 59 and a half years old. When determining the kind of account to which you will make contributions, it is important to give serious consideration to your requirements and objectives.

Balancing Roth and Traditional Accounts: Managing Tax Liability in Retirement

Having a mix of Roth and traditional retirement accounts can provide several advantages when it comes to managing tax liability in retirement. Here are some of the potential advantages:

- Diversification of tax treatment: By having both Roth and traditional retirement accounts, you can diversify your tax treatment in retirement. Roth accounts provide tax-free withdrawals, while traditional accounts provide tax-deferred growth and taxable withdrawals. This can help you better manage your tax liability in retirement and potentially reduce your overall tax burden.
- Flexibility in retirement income planning: With a mix of Roth and traditional accounts, you have greater flexibility in how you withdraw retirement income in retirement. You can choose to withdraw from your traditional accounts to take advantage of lower tax brackets while using your Roth accounts for tax-free income. This can help you optimize your retirement income and minimize your tax liability.

- Protection against changing tax laws: Tax laws can change over time, and having a mix of Roth and traditional accounts can protect against these changes. For example, if tax rates increase in the future, having tax-free income from your Roth accounts can provide a buffer against higher taxes.
- Estate planning benefits: Roth accounts can provide estate planning benefits by allowing you to pass on tax-free income to your heirs. This can help you maximize the value of your estate and potentially reduce the tax burden for your beneficiaries.

Having a combination of regular and Roth retirement accounts does, however, come with the possibility of several drawbacks, which should be noted as an essential point. For example, Roth accounts have contribution limits and income eligibility requirements that may limit your ability to contribute. Additionally, withdrawals from Roth accounts may be subject to penalties and taxes if certain rules are not followed.

The choice of whether or not to have a combination of Roth and standard retirement accounts will, in the end, be determined by your unique financial status as well as the objectives you want to achieve during retirement. It is essential to speak with a financial counselor to ascertain the approach that is most suitable for your requirements.

Incorporating Roth Accounts: Evaluating Your Overall Retirement Income Strategy

One of the most crucial aspects of retirement preparation is the individual's approach to generating money in their golden years. Factors including their existing tax situation, their intended lifestyle, and their expected income all need to be taken into account. One important choice to make is whether to make contributions to a standard account, such as a traditional 401(k) or traditional IRA, or a Roth account, such as a Roth 401(k) or Roth IRA.

Although Roth accounts have the potential to provide several benefits, such as tax-free growth and tax-free withdrawals in retirement, it is essential to understand how these funds might be incorporated into your overall plan for generating income. If you anticipate being in a tax bracket that is higher in retirement than the one you are in now, it may make sense to contribute to a Roth account since you will pay taxes on your contributions at the tax rate that you are now paying, which is likely to be lower. This may decrease the impact of RMDs from traditional accounts and make it simpler for you to manage your tax liability during retirement.

On the other hand, making contributions to a conventional account might be more beneficial if you anticipate being in a lower tax band than you currently are. This is because you may get a tax break on your contributions right now, and you'll pay an even lower tax rate on your withdrawals after you're retired. This may be particularly helpful if you anticipate having a considerable amount of taxable income in retirement, such as from Social Security payments or pensions. Other potential sources of such income include stock dividends and interest income.

It is also crucial to analyze the entire sources of your retirement income and how those sources can affect your tax status after retirement. Contributions you make to a Roth account, for instance, may affect the portion of your Social Security payments that is subject to taxation if you intend to depend significantly on those benefits during retirement. In addition, if you want to continue working on a part-time basis or launch a small company when you retire, this may increase your taxable income and, thus, your tax burden.

If you have a certain income target in mind for your retirement years, it is imperative that you investigate all of the potential routes toward realizing that target. If you believe you will be in a higher tax band in retirement, or if you just want more control over how your money is taxed, a Roth IRA may be a smart option for you. Contributing to a conventional account, on the other hand, maybe the more advantageous choice if you are now subject to a higher tax rate but anticipate being subject to a lower tax band when you reach retirement age.

Remember that your strategy for retirement income should be comprehensive, including a wide range of potential revenue streams like Social Security, pensions, rental income, and the sale of assets. You may assist assure a more stable and secure retirement for yourself by bringing in money from a variety of sources.

Your specific circumstances, as well as your long-term plan for generating income throughout retirement, should serve as the primary considerations to guide your final choice on whether to put money into a regular or a Roth IRA. It may be good to contact a financial counselor or tax specialist to assist you in determining the technique that is most appropriate for your circumstances.

Personal Work Sheet

Tax Efficiency Analysis

Taxed Currently		Taxed Later		Taxed Never*	
Checking/Savings	$__________	IRAs, SEP IRAs	$__________	Roth IRAs/401 (k)	$__________
CDs	$__________	SIMPLE IRAs 401 (k), 403 (B)	$__________	Municipal Bonds	$__________
Stock Mutual Funds	$__________			Universal Life Insurance	$__________
Bond Mutual Funds	$__________	Pension Plans	$__________	Whole Life Insurance	$__________
Stocks	$__________	Variable Annuities	$__________		
Bonds	$__________	Fixed Annuities	$__________	529 College Plans	$__________
UGMA	$__________	Savings Bonds	$__________	Coverdale Education IRA	$__________
Other	$__________	Other	$__________	Other	$__________
Current Total	$__________	Current Total	$__________	Current Total	$__________
	__________%		__________%		__________%

Are Your Investments Increasing or Decreasing Your Tax Burden?

1. Tax Deductible?
2. Tax Deferred?
3. Tax Free?

*Certain Events and distributions may be subject to taxation and individuals would be responsible for the appropriate liability. 1099s may be required for informational purposes only, under certain circumstances. This piece provides general information regarding the Internal Revenue Code and does not take into consideration specific state laws.

Haye P. (2015)

Chapter 4

UNDERSTANDING PERMANENT LIFE INSURANCE

When it comes to life insurance, there are two primary types: term and permanent. Unlike term life insurance, which provides coverage for a set period, permanent life insurance covers the policyholder for their entire life. This means that if the policyholder dies while premiums are still being paid, the beneficiary will receive the death benefit.

Permanent life insurance comes in different forms, including variable universal life (VUL), whole life (WL), custom whole life (CWL), and indexed universal life (IUL). Each type of policy has its unique features and benefits, making it essential to do some research to determine which one is best for your specific needs and aspirations.

One advantage of permanent life insurance is that it can accumulate cash value over time. The policyholder can withdraw or borrow against the cash value or use it to pay premiums. Gains in cash value are not taxed until the funds are withdrawn, making it a tax-advantaged investment option.

Moreover, permanent life insurance can provide financial security for future generations. The lifelong nature of the insurance means that it may be left to loved ones free of gift and estate taxes. This makes it a valuable tool for estate planning and wealth transfer.

However, it's worth noting that obtaining permanent life insurance requires the approval of a life insurance provider. In most cases, a medical exam is required as part of the approval procedure, which also includes a review of the applicant's health history and any relevant risk factors.

When it comes to saving for retirement, providing for a family's financial security, and accumulating wealth, permanent life insurance can be an invaluable instrument. With its tax benefits, cash value accumulation, and estate planning advantages, it's no wonder why so many individuals choose permanent life insurance as a part of their overall financial strategy. As a financial advisor with years of experience in the field, I highly recommend exploring this option to determine if it's right for you.

Life Insurance: The Rock of Retirement

The Perfect Source of Extra Money

Retirement income planning may be difficult to understand and implement. There is a plethora of investment opportunities that are touted by financial consultants, each with its own set of potential benefits and drawbacks. However, life insurance stands out as an often-overlooked tool that may protect against many of these dangers.

Retirement income planning that involves life insurance is more sophisticated financial planning. Life insurance salespeople tend to be enthusiastic about this tactic, whereas stock market fans tend to regard it with disdain. It's possible, nevertheless, that life insurance offers certain advantages not seen elsewhere. We need to give this idea another look, maybe.

Exposing the Hidden Nature of Danger

In spite of its importance, many of us lack a firm grasp of the idea of risk, despite its centrality to sound financial planning. We tend to be optimistic people. Thus, we tend to downplay the significance of the risks we face on a regular basis.

Risk in the financial sector is seen as a continuum. Losing a wager at a slot machine in Las Vegas is an example of a risk that can be readily measured. Complex hazards, such as the possibility that your home could burn down within the next five years, are on the opposite end of the spectrum. Due to their complexity, these hazards are notoriously difficult to quantify precisely.

Planning for retirement has its own special dangers. Market, interest rate, system, and liquidity risks are all examples that most financial advisers will address openly with their clients. Longevity risk, cash flow risk, and retirement timing risk, on the other hand, are not as well recognized but yet have a major impact.

The truth of the risk associated with when one decides to retire is sobering. The time span between when you start working and when you retire is fixed. And that number of years is a major factor in determining your retirement security. Even if you do everything by the book, an unexpected drop in the stock market may ruin your retirement savings in a flash.

The Bear Market's Damaging Effect on Retirement Savings

Year	Withdrawal	Annual Yield	Remaining Balance
1	$ (50,000.00)	-35%	$ 617,500.00
2	$ (50,000.00)	-15%	$ 482,375.00
3	$ (50,000.00)	15%	$ 497,231.25
4	$ (50,000.00)	20%	$ 536,677.50
5	$ (50,000.00)	-18%	$ 399,075.55
6	$ (50,000.00)	30%	$ 453,798.22
7	$ (50,000.00)	15%	$ 464,367.95
8	$ (50,000.00)	-25%	$ 310,775.96
9	$ (50,000.00)	26%	$ 328,577.71
10	$ (50,000.00)	35%	$ 376,079.91
11	$ (50,000.00)	20%	$ 391,295.89
12	$ (50,000.00)	-18%	$ 279,862.63
13	$ (50,000.00)	45%	$ 333,300.81
14	$ (50,000.00)	4%	$ 294,632.85
15	$ (50,000.00)	-18%	$ 200,598.93
16	$ (50,000.00)	6%	$ 159,634.87
17	$ (50,000.00)	-20%	$ 87,707.90
18	$ (50,000.00)	35%	$ 50,905.66
19	$ (50,000.00)	20%	$ 1,086.79
20	$ (50,000.00)	15%	$ (56,250.19)

Think of the havoc a bear market may wreak if it hit during your early retirement years. Consider a $1,000,000 retirement account that yields $50,000 per year at the recommended 5% withdrawal rate.

To show how market swings might affect this portfolio, we'll examine two what-if scenarios in which the identical set of yearly yields over a 20-year period is used, but in the opposite order. In both cases, the average yearly return is 6.85%, which is a realistic forecast given the market's track record.

Year	Withdrawal	Annual Yield	Remaining Balance
1	$ (50,000.00)	15%	$ 1,092,500.00
2	$ (50,000.00)	20%	$ 1,251,000.00
3	$ (50,000.00)	35%	$ 1,621,350.00
4	$ (50,000.00)	-20%	$ 1,257,080.00
5	$ (50,000.00)	6%	$ 1,279,504.80
6	$ (50,000.00)	-18%	$ 1,008,193.94
7	$ (50,000.00)	4%	$ 996,521.69
8	$ (50,000.00)	45%	$ 1,372,456.46
9	$ (50,000.00)	-18%	$ 1,084,414.29
10	$ (50,000.00)	20%	$ 1,241,297.15
11	$ (50,000.00)	35%	$ 1,608,251.16
12	$ (50,000.00)	26%	$ 1,963,396.46
13	$ (50,000.00)	-25%	$ 1,435,047.34
14	$ (50,000.00)	15%	$ 1,592,804.44
15	$ (50,000.00)	30%	$ 2,005,645.78
16	$ (50,000.00)	-18%	$ 1,603,629.54
17	$ (50,000.00)	20%	$ 1,864,355.44
18	$ (50,000.00)	15%	$ 2,086,508.76
19	$ (50,000.00)	-15%	$ 1,731,032.45
20	$ (50,000.00)	-35%	$ 1,092,671.09

Bullish Market

In the first scenario, the market is bullish from the outset. The portfolio is still strong despite experiencing a couple of bear markets and some big market downturns at the conclusion. Thanks to market growth, the account balance is still well over a million dollars 20 years after the first investment.

The returns are switched around in the second case. However, the portfolio ran out of money a year before the 20-year milestone since the bear market arrived a year earlier than expected. This exemplifies the disastrous impact that retirement timing risk may have.

Year	Withdrawal	Annual Yield	Remaining Balance
1	$ (50,000.00)	2%	$ 969,000.00
2	$ (50,000.00)	2%	$ 937,380.00
3	$ (50,000.00)	2%	$ 905,127.60
4	$ (50,000.00)	2%	$ 872,230.15
5	$ (50,000.00)	2%	$ 838,674.76
6	$ (50,000.00)	2%	$ 804,448.25
7	$ (50,000.00)	2%	$ 769,537.22
8	$ (50,000.00)	2%	$ 733,927.96
9	$ (50,000.00)	2%	$ 697,606.52
10	$ (50,000.00)	2%	$ 660,558.65
11	$ (50,000.00)	2%	$ 622,769.82
12	$ (50,000.00)	2%	$ 584,225.22
13	$ (50,000.00)	2%	$ 544,909.72
14	$ (50,000.00)	2%	$ 504,807.92
15	$ (50,000.00)	2%	$ 463,904.08
16	$ (50,000.00)	2%	$ 422,182.16
17	$ (50,000.00)	2%	$ 379,625.80
18	$ (50,000.00)	2%	$ 336,218.32
19	$ (50,000.00)	2%	$ 291,942.68
20	$ (50,000.00)	2%	$ 246,781.54

Bearish Market

The Rock in a Rough Sea: Why You Need Life Insurance

Life insurance comes into play since it is a low-risk asset that is particularly effective at generating income because it is not affected by market fluctuations.

Let's go back to the first example and plug in an annual rate of 2 percent for all the potential yields. The predictable income from a life insurance policy is mimicked here. The retiree, in this case, not only survives the whole 20 years but also has around $250,000 in savings at the end of it all.

Whole life, current assumption universal life, and indexed universal life insurance all provide steady income because of the security their underlying death benefits provide. These regulations stay much below the industry norm for years, avoiding even the somewhat detrimental ones. Let's assume a comfortable 6.85% annualized return over a 20-year period, as reported by the majority of large mutual fund firms.

Using this information, let's investigate two possibilities. A bull market exists during the first three years of the first scenario, followed by a few bear markets and then severe bear markets towards the conclusion. We still end up with $1,092,671.09 at the conclusion of the 20-year period, despite the weak markets, thanks to the initial strong performance of the market and subsequent market gains.

In the second case, though, we only switch around the sequence of returns. The bear markets this time around have started earlier than usual, but the average return hasn't changed much. A year before the conclusion of the 20-year term, we run out of money in this scenario.

This fictitious scenario illustrates retirement timing risk, sometimes known as the danger of losing money in the market at the wrong time. A market slump at the wrong moment might have a major impact on our retirement savings.

The Role of Life Insurance in Reducing the Risk of Delaying Retirement

The low-risk nature of life insurance makes it a useful instrument for generating retirement income. It's worth is that it can't be affected by market downturns.

Year	Withdrawal	Annual Yield	Remaining Balance
1	$ (50,000.00)	2%	$ 969,000.00
2	$ (50,000.00)	2%	$ 937,380.00
3	$ (50,000.00)	2%	$ 905,127.60
4	$ (50,000.00)	2%	$ 872,230.15
5	$ (50,000.00)	2%	$ 838,674.76
6	$ (50,000.00)	2%	$ 804,448.25
7	$ (50,000.00)	2%	$ 769,537.22
8	$ (50,000.00)	2%	$ 733,927.96
9	$ (50,000.00)	2%	$ 697,606.52
10	$ (50,000.00)	2%	$ 660,558.65
11	$ (50,000.00)	2%	$ 622,769.82
12	$ (50,000.00)	2%	$ 584,225.22
13	$ (50,000.00)	2%	$ 544,909.72
14	$ (50,000.00)	2%	$ 504,807.92
15	$ (50,000.00)	2%	$ 463,904.08
16	$ (50,000.00)	2%	$ 422,182.16
17	$ (50,000.00)	2%	$ 379,625.80
18	$ (50,000.00)	2%	$ 336,218.32
19	$ (50,000.00)	2%	$ 291,942.68
20	$ (50,000.00)	2%	$ 246,781.54

Life Insurance Static Return

To see this in action, let's go back to our original example, but this time, assume a 2% annual return in lieu of all the hypothetical yearly returns. Our retiree here not only makes it through the whole 20 years but also emerges with an additional $246,781.54 in savings.

If you invest $1,000,000 and earn 2% per year forever, and remove $50,000 annually, you won't run out of money in 20 years, even if you don't touch the principal. This is an undeniable fact of mathematics.

Whole life, current assumption universal life, and indexed universal life insurance all provide stability since they are not affected by big or moderate negative returns. Life insurance is a useful retirement income strategy since it provides financial security and improves your potential to create income at any time.

The steady flow of money from life insurance is a good source of income. Time risk, which may have a significant impact on your retirement savings, is one of the hazards it avoids. Because of this, life insurance is a serious financial tool that should be considered while planning for a comfortable retirement.

Use The Term LIRP/SLIRP For Permanent Life Policies

A technique known as Supplemental Life Insurance Retirement Planning (SLIRP) involves purchasing permanent life insurance to accumulate retirement funds that are exempt from taxes. It includes acquiring a permanent life insurance policy, which is often a kind of universal life insurance, and then overfunding the policy with premium payments that are higher than the amount required to keep the death benefit at its current level.

The insurance allows the surplus premiums to grow tax-deferred while also contributing to the policy's rising cash value over time. Policy loans and withdrawals from the cash value of the insurance are typically tax-free up to the amount of the premiums paid (Indexed Universal Life (IUL) vs. 401k). In this manner, the LIRP/SLIRP technique may be used to offer a stream of income that is exempt from taxation during retirement.

When utilized in combination with other retirement savings vehicles, such as regular IRAs or 401(k) plans, the LIRP/SLIRP method may help diversify retirement income and offer extra income that is exempt from taxes throughout retirement. It is also possible to utilize it to transfer wealth to beneficiaries in a tax-effective manner, which is another purpose for it.

Although LIRP/SLIRP may provide considerable tax advantages and the possibility of increased income during retirement, it is essential to give serious consideration to the costs and risks that are connected with permanent life insurance plans. When compared to term life insurance, the premiums and expenses associated with these plans are often much higher. Additionally, the investment returns may not be as great as those associated with alternative investment choices. In addition, accessing the cash value of the policy via policy loans or withdrawals might diminish the death benefit and put the long-term sustainability of the policy in jeopardy. It is essential to collaborate with a financial adviser or insurance expert who is familiar with the LIRP/SLIRP approach and can assist you in determining whether or not it is an appropriate choice for meeting the requirements of your retirement planning.

How Permanent Life Insurance Can Help Build Wealth And Generate Income

Permanent life insurance can help build wealth and generate income in several ways:

1) Cash value accumulation: A portion of the premium paid into a permanent life insurance policy goes towards building cash value over time. The cash value accumulates tax-free and may be withdrawn or used as a loan if necessary. Depending on the policy, the cash value can also earn interest or dividends, which can further enhance its growth potential.
2) Tax-free income: Since withdrawals from the cash value of a permanent life insurance policy are considered a return of premium and not taxable income, they can provide tax-free income during retirement. Those who have already contributed the maximum allowed to other tax-deferred retirement accounts may benefit greatly from this.
3) Estate planning: Estate planning is another important application for permanent life insurance. In most cases, the death benefit is not subject to income tax, and in certain cases, it may not be subject to estate tax either. This can help ensure that loved ones are taken care of, and assets are passed on efficiently.
4) Protection against market downturns: Permanent life insurance policies, such as indexed universal life, can offer downside protection in the event of market downturns. Since these policies are

tied to a market index, they can provide a floor of protection while still offering the potential for gains.

5. Collateral for loans: For those in need of quick access to finance for business or investment possibilities, the cash value of a permanent life insurance policy may be utilized as collateral for loans.
6. Non-direct recognition – This is a feature that allows policyholders to borrow money from their policy without affecting the interest earned on the cash value. When you take a loan from your policy, the non-direct recognition feature allows you to continue earning interest as if the borrowed money was still in the policy.

For example, if you take a loan at 5% interest and your policy earns 10% interest, the policy will continue to earn the 10% interest rate even though you have withdrawn funds from it. This feature can be advantageous for policyholders, as it enables them to access their cash value without sacrificing the growth of their policy. See visual representation:

Direct Recognition
Bank
100,000 on Deposit
C 10% interest
90,000 Withdrawal
10,000 left is $1,000 Interest

Non-Direct Recognition
LIRP
$100,000 on Deposit
C 10% interest
$90,000 Withdrawal
$10,000 left is $10,000 Interest

The rates for permanent life insurance are often greater than those for term life insurance, despite the former's numerous advantages. It's also possible that the cash value's investment returns won't measure up to those of other investment options. It's important to carefully consider one's financial goals and needs before deciding on a permanent life insurance policy.

For Your Life And Generational Wealth. Examples Of Who Uses SLIRP

Presidents, Banks, CEOs, Disney, JC Penny, Rockefeller

Permanent life insurance, more precisely SLIRP, may be used not only for the preparation for retirement but also for the accumulation of wealth and the transmission of family heritage to the next generations. The purchaser of a perpetual life insurance policy can build up cash value over the course of the policy's duration, which then becomes available for use in the form of loans or withdrawals. This may offer a source of liquid assets that can be used in times of crisis or to take advantage of possibilities, such as buying a house or paying for a child's education. In addition, beneficiaries of permanent life insurance plans may receive tax-free income from the death benefit of the policy. These funds can be used toward the payment of estate taxes, the support of loved ones, or the establishment of a charitable legacy.

Beneficiaries

Supplemental Life Insurance Retirement Plans (SLIRP) are used by individuals and organizations for various reasons, including wealth accumulation, tax-free income, and legacy planning. Here are some examples of who uses SLIRP:

1. High net worth individuals: LIRP/SLIRP can be an attractive option for individuals with high net worth who are looking to grow and protect their wealth. The tax benefits of SLIRP, along with the ability to accumulate wealth over time, make it a popular choice among high-net-worth individuals.
2. Business owners: LIRP/SLIRP can also be used as a business planning tool. Business owners can use LIRP/SLIRP to fund buy-

sell agreements, key person insurance, and executive compensation plans.

3. Banks and financial institutions: The LIRP/SLIRP is often used by banks and other financial organizations as a means of funding employee benefit schemes such as deferred payment plans and executive bonus plans.
4. Corporations: Large corporations, such as Disney and JCPenney, have used LIRP/SLIRP to fund their executive compensation plans and employee benefit programs.
5. Celebrities and athletes: LIRP/SLIRP can also be used by celebrities and athletes to protect their wealth and provide for their families in the event of their untimely death.
6. Politicians and public figures: It's not uncommon for politicians and public figures to use LIRP/SLIRP as part of their estate planning and legacy planning strategies.
7. Wealthy families: Finally, LIRP/SLIRP can be an effective tool for generational wealth planning. By using LIRP/SLIRP, wealthy families can provide for their heirs and ensure their legacy continues for generations to come. The Rockefeller family is a notable example of a family that has used LIRP/SLIRP to preserve their wealth and legacy.

Overall, LIRP/SLIRP is a versatile financial tool that can be used by individuals and organizations across a variety of industries for wealth accumulation, income generation, and legacy planning.

Many prominent individuals and organizations have recognized the financial benefits of LIRP/SLIRP:

• Former President Franklin Roosevelt had a cash value of $576,000 in his policy upon his death. In today's money, that would be worth approximately $8.5 million.

• Prominent families and individuals, such as the Rockefellers, the Kennedys, and even business giants like McDonald's, have owned LIRP/SLIRP policies. Senator John McCain notably used his policy's cash value to fund his political campaign.

• Even Walt Disney benefited from LIRP/SLIRP, as he borrowed from his policy's cash value to fund the creation of Disneyland. During the Great Depression, JC Penny did the same to keep his business afloat.

• Financial industry professionals, including bankers, Wall Street executives, and Fortune 1000 executives, also commonly own LIRP/SLIRP. Interestingly, 57% of brokers managing equity funds do not own the funds they sell, but they do hold large life insurance policies.

• Banks, too, invest heavily in LIRP/SLIRP. Out of approximately 4,000 banks, they collectively own $160 billion in LIRP/SLIRP. For instance, Bank of America owns $22 billion in LIRP/SLIRP, an amount exceeding the total value of all their 5600 branches and even their Manhattan skyscraper combined. Other major banks like Citibank, JP Morgan Chase, and Wells Fargo have billions invested in LIRP/SLIRP as well. In fact, for 68% of all banks, LIRP/SLIRP is their most significant asset.

• Corporations also use LIRP/SLIRP in unique ways. For example, General Electric (GE) used a LIRP/SLIRP policy to pay Jack Welch's pension. When he died in 2020, GE recovered all their money via the tax-free death benefit from his policy.

• Finally, even former Federal Reserve Chair Ben Bernanke is a believer. He has invested 85% of his total wealth in life insurance and annuity products from life insurance companies.

These are some highlights of the broad appeal and financial utility of LIRP/SLIRP for both individuals and organizations alike.

Chapter 5

Building Retirement Income with Permanent Life Insurance

Imagine sailing into your golden years with a financial strategy that not only boosts your retirement income but also shields your loved ones. Enter SLIRP, the Supplemental Life Insurance Retirement Plan. It transforms permanent life insurance policies, like whole life, universal life, or indexed universal life, into a powerhouse for building cash value to fund your retirement dreams.

Picture this: tax-free growth of your cash value, tax-free withdrawals, and loans. With permanent life insurance, you can enjoy your retirement without fretting about tax bills. Wave goodbye to the fear of market volatility, as your policy's cash value remains steadfast even in turbulent times.

Embarking on this journey starts with purchasing a policy and diligently making premium payments. As time goes by, your policy accumulates cash value, ready to be tapped during retirement via withdrawals or loans. Bonus? A guaranteed death benefit to safeguard your beneficiaries.

But wait, there's more! Retirement with permanent life insurance brings a myriad of income-generation avenues. The rising cash value is your tax-free treasure chest, accessible whenever needed. Or, convert your policy's death benefit into a steady income stream by selling it to an investor or using it as collateral for a loan.

Some policies, like indexed universal life (IUL), boast an "income rider" option. This nifty addition guarantees a tax-free income in retirement, providing a sense of financial security.

Like any great adventure, planning is crucial. Consult a financial expert to see if this path is right for your unique situation and objectives. Explore policy conditions, premiums, and other costs to make an informed decision.

In a nutshell, permanent life insurance can be a game-changer for your retirement. With tax-free income and protection for your loved ones, it could be your key to unlocking a comfortable and worry-free retirement. Just remember to partner with a financial expert to ensure your plan is tailored to your goals and resources. Happy retirement planning!

Non-Direct Recognition And How That Is An Amazing Tool

Picture this: you're navigating the world of mutual insurance and stumble upon direct and non-direct recognition. What's the difference, and why does it matter?

Direct recognition, as its name suggests, directly affects your dividend rates when you borrow against your policy's cash value. It's like your insurance company is watching your every move, adjusting the rates accordingly. Non-direct recognition, on the other hand, is the incognito mode of the insurance world. Borrowing from your policy's cash value doesn't influence dividend rates, so everyone enjoys the same rate, regardless of outstanding loans.

Permanent life insurance plans, like whole life and indexed universal life, often come with non-direct recognition. It's a nifty feature that lets you take a policy loan without stunting your policy's cash value growth earnings.

Direct recognition may feel like a tightrope walk, where borrowing impacts your policy's dividends or interest credit. But don't be fooled; non-direct recognition companies have their own ways of leveling the playing field. If there's a mismatch between the total return and loan interest, they may either subsidize the disconnection or offer a non-direct recognition loan with a higher interest rate.

For example, when the Federal Reserve increased interest rates in 2022 and 2023, non-direct recognition loan rates soared from 3% to over 5.7%.

But the reality behind one of the most widely-held misconceptions about unlimited banking is that: you're not paying interest to yourself when you borrow against your whole life insurance policy. The insurance company lends you money from their general investment account, while your policy's cash value acts as collateral. It's a team effort, with your policy continually compounding and working in your favor.

At certain times (like the present), some whole-life policies benefit from taking out a loan. And that's the hidden gem of non-direct recognition loans in the ever-evolving world of insurance.

LIRP/SLIRP As The Foundation Of Any Financial Plan

This kind of insurance plan often comes with specific guarantees, such as a guaranteed minimum interest rate or a guaranteed death benefit, which may help offer a certain degree of financial certainty. For example, a guaranteed minimum interest rate.

Inflation protection is a feature that may be included in some permanent life insurance plans. This feature may assist in ensuring that the policy's value is preserved throughout the course of its duration. The success of these insurance policies may depend on the success of the stock market or other assets, so it is important to remember that there is always some risk involved.

Individuals can produce income throughout retirement by utilizing a permanent life insurance policy as the cornerstone of their financial strategy. In addition, the death benefit that is passed on to the individual's heirs is exempt from taxation. This strategy is often referred to as Supplemental Life Insurance Retirement Planning (SLIRP), which is an abbreviation for the full acronym. However, before making any judgments on these kinds of policies, it is essential to give thorough consideration to both the costs and the advantages of these options. Consult a financial expert to help you plan your financial future. Working with a financial professional is also crucial since they can assist and guide you through the process.

The advantages of LIRP/SLIRP extend well beyond the tax realm. It provides inflation protection through the cash value's potential to expand over time, and it assures a death payout and cash value buildup. The flexibility of LIRP/SLIRP means that the policyholder may take some calculated risks while investing.

In the end, the sort of permanent life insurance policy that is appropriate for a LIRP/SLIRP will be determined by the specific financial circumstances and objectives of a person. It is essential to collaborate with a financial expert who can assist in evaluating your requirements and providing direction about the choice of the appropriate coverage.

Tax Benefits of Using Permanent Life Insurance

Using permanent life insurance as a source of income throughout retirement comes with several favorable tax implications. To begin, the cash value that is included in a permanent life insurance policy grows tax-deferred. The cash value appreciation is not taxable until the funds are taken from the insurance policy. Because of this, your insurance can amass greater money over time.

Second, if you make a withdrawal of money from your insurance, you are exempt from paying taxes on those funds up to the total amount of premiums you have paid. Because the premiums for a life insurance policy are paid with money that was earned after taxes, the Internal Revenue Service considers those dollars to have already been subject to taxation.

Third, if you take out a policy loan rather than a withdrawal, the money from the loan is typically not considered taxable income as long as the loan is kept within specific limitations and the policy is kept active. This is the case even if the money is taken out of the policy. In your retirement years, this might offer you a stream of cash that is exempt from taxation.

Finally, if you pass away and your beneficiaries get the death benefit from your life insurance policy, they are normally exempt from paying income tax on that benefit. This is because the payout is considered a death benefit. This may be a crucial component of estate planning and can assist in guaranteeing that your heirs get the full benefit of the life insurance policy that you have purchased for them.

Overall, utilizing permanent life insurance as a means to generate income during retirement can offer various tax benefits that help you keep more of your money in your golden years. Nonetheless, it's crucial to consult with a financial expert to comprehend the tax implications of any strategy and ensure that the approach aligns with your broader financial goals.

In reference to permanent life insurance policies "unlimited amounts of money can be contributed into Permanent Insurances plans every year" which means that there is no constraint on the number of funds that can be deposited into these policies annually. It's a reference to the fact that premiums for variable universal life insurance may be set at any level. Unlike retirement accounts like IRAs and 401(k)s, permanent life insurance policies do not have yearly contribution restrictions.

It is claimed that a permanent life insurance policy's cash value is "fully liquid" if its owners may access it whenever they choose without incurring any fees. The policyholder has entire control over the cash value and may use it in any way they see fit, including withdrawing it from the policy or using it as collateral for loans.

Finally, "has no income limits" means that everyone, regardless of income, may make premium payments on a permanent life insurance policy. Unlike other retirement accounts, such as Roth IRAs, which restrict contributions and determine eligibility based on a person's yearly income, this one does not.

Due to its attractive tax benefits, including tax-free growth and tax-free withdrawals in retirement, permanent life insurance policies are a popular option for people looking to generate income during their golden years. Additionally, there are no limits on contributions or earnings, so you may put as much money as you like into the account. Because of this, they are a good option for those who face barriers to contributing to traditional retirement accounts. It's important to remember, too, that permanent life insurance rates and deductibles may be much higher than those of other retirement savings options. Therefore, before deciding to use this insurance as a means of earning income during retirement, it is crucial to carefully weigh the pros and downsides of doing so.

Exploring the Option of Accessing Funds: Line of Credit Loan Against Life Insurance Coverage

Taking out a loan or line of credit against the cash value of a permanent life insurance policy is one of the policy's most powerful features. This option gives policyholders access to an additional, potentially advantageous retirement income stream.

What is a Loan Against Life Insurance Coverage?

A policy loan, also known as a loan against a life insurance policy, is a loan that may be taken out against a permanent life insurance policy. Your policy's cash value will be used as collateral for the loan, and you'll be able to take out a loan of up to the policy's entire cash value.

When Does It Activate?

A loan against life insurance is a loan given by an insurance company based on the cash value of a policy. You are free to put these monies to whatever purpose you see fit. You may choose how and when you want to pay back the loan. If you haven't paid back the loan in full by the time of your death, your heirs will have to pay back the principal and interest on the debt.

Why are there Benefits?

The favorable tax treatment of life insurance loans is the key benefit. Loans taken out against a permanent life insurance policy are currently not treated as taxable income. This feature is especially useful in retirement when careful management of taxable income might affect the taxation of Social Security benefits and Medicare premium expenses since it allows you to withdraw cash value without raising taxable income.

The low-interest rate is just another perk of this loan. A life insurance loan might be a good alternative to a personal loan or a credit card loan because of its reduced interest rate.

Lastly, another benefit of a life insurance loan is its adaptability. There is no set timeline for making payments, unlike with most loans. In retirement, when income is less stable, this may be a huge boon to freedom of choice.

What are the Considerations?

There are benefits to borrowing against a life insurance policy, but there are also risks to think about. For instance, a lapsed insurance might result in a hefty tax bill if the sum of the loan and interest payments exceeds the policy's cash value.

In addition, timely loan repayment is recommended but not required. This is because the loan's interest might accumulate, cutting down the money your loved ones would get if you died.

Planning for Retirement: How to Include This Approach?

If you know how to utilize a life insurance loan wisely, you may improve your plan for retirement income. If you are at a higher tax rate because of your other income, you may choose to withdraw money from your life insurance policy instead of your IRA or 401(k) in that year.

Financial adaptability and potential tax benefits are only two of the many benefits that may be gained by taking out a line of credit loan against life insurance. To see how this tactic fits into your entire retirement income strategy, it is recommended that you see a financial counselor. It's a method of maximizing the tax benefits and retirement income from a permanent life insurance policy.

Chapter 6

PENSION MAXIMIZATION

Getting The Most Income For You And Your Spouse

The goal of pension maximizing, a kind of retirement planning, is to maximize the amount of money you and your spouse get in retirement. Common users include those with pension plans that may be cashed out in either a single life payment or a joint and survivor payment.

With a single life payout, the pensioner's spouse receives no money after their passing. A joint and survivor payment, on the other hand, reduces the pensioner's payout during life but maintains it, at the same or a reduced rate, during the spouse's lifetime.

The difference between the single life payment and the joint and survivor payout may be covered by permanent life insurance as part of a pension maximizing strategy. The pensioner buys a life insurance policy whose death benefit is at least as large as the disparity between the single life payment and the joint and survivor payout. This not only ensures that the pensioner's spouse will get a death benefit sufficient to replace the lost pension income but also provides the pensioner with a higher monthly income throughout their lifetime.

The pensioner's higher lifetime income helps pay for the life insurance policy, and the surviving spouse receives a tax-free death benefit.

However, the expense of the life insurance payments has to be weighed against the gains from the larger pension. Selecting a reliable and solvent life insurance provider is also crucial for the timely distribution of the death benefit.

Understanding Pension Plans

A pension plan is a specific kind of retirement plan that is offered by an organization to workers in order to ensure that they will have a steady income once they reach retirement age. Employee contributions to the plan are generally done on a tax-deferred basis and may be made in addition to employer payments.

The most common kinds of pension plans are those with defined benefits and those with defined contributions.

A pension plan known as a defined benefit plan is one in which the employer commits to pay a certain monthly benefit to the employee upon retirement. An employee's salary and length of service to the firm are included in the calculation used to determine this benefit. The employer is the one that is responsible for investing the contributions and takes on all of the risk associated with how those contributions perform in the market.

A pension plan known as a defined contribution plan is one in which the employee and/or the employer make contributions to an individual account for the employee, and the employee is responsible for investing the contributions that have been made. The value of the account, when the retiree takes it out of service, determines how much money they get as retirement income.

Pension plans may either be fully funded, which means that the employer has contributed sufficient funds to the plan to pay all future pension liabilities, or they can be partly funded, which means that the employer has not contributed sufficient funds to completely cover future obligations.

There is also the possibility that pension plans may be subject to vesting requirements. These are rules that establish how much of the employer's contributions the employee is entitled to receive if they leave the firm before they retire. There are two different ways that vesting may take place: it can be immediate, in which case the employee is immediately entitled to all of the contributions made by the employer, or it can be progressive, in which case the employee will gradually become increasingly entitled to the contributions as time goes on.

In general, pension plans may be a significant component of an employee's retirement planning since they provide a source of guaranteed income after the individual has left active employment. However, it is important to know the kind of plan that is being given, the current financial health of the plan, and the requirements for vesting in order to have a thorough grasp of the various benefits and restrictions.

Factors To Consider When Maximizing Your Pension

When it comes to maximizing your pension, there are several factors to consider, including:

Pension payout options:

When trying to get the most out of your pension, one of the most crucial considerations to make is whether or not your plan provides a variety of different payout alternatives. Depending on the plan, participants may be able to choose from a variety of payment alternatives, such as single-life, joint, survivor, or period specific. You and your spouse need to give careful thought to the subject of which option is best for you since each has its own perks and downsides.

Pension vesting:

Your pension plan's vesting timeline is another important aspect to take into consideration. The period that you must work for a firm before you are eligible to collect the full pension benefits is referred to as the "vesting" time requirement. Knowing the vesting schedule for your plan is essential, as it might affect your ability to save for retirement and whether or not you decide to stay with your current employer.

Pension contribution limits:

If your pension plan allows for contributions, it is essential that you have a solid understanding of the contribution limitations and evaluate whether or not you are contributing the maximum amount possible to the plan. You may assist in guaranteeing that you obtain the most benefit from the plan when you retire by making contributions that are as high as feasible.

Pension funding status:

When trying to get the most out of your pension, another essential aspect to take into consideration is the financial state of your pension plan. This determines whether the plan is fully financed or underfunded and whether it is fully funded or underfunded might influence the plan's capacity to pay out benefits in the future. It's crucial that you know how your plan is funded at all times and whether there have been any changes that might affect your benefits.

Pension benefit formulas:

When you retire, the amount of benefits you get from your pension plan might be affected by the benefit formula that is employed by the plan. It is possible to make educated judgments regarding your retirement planning if you have a solid understanding of how the formula operates and whether or not it is advantageous to you.

Pension plan changes:

Last but not least, it is essential that you be informed of any changes to your pension plan that may affect the benefits you get. Alterations to the benefit formula, the vesting schedule, or the payment options may fall under this category. Keeping abreast of any developments will assist you in adapting your retirement plans to accommodate the new circumstances.

You may make the most of the benefits you get from your pension and guarantee a pleasant retirement if you take these considerations into account and collaborate with a financial counselor or retirement planner.

Pension Maximization Strategies

Pension maximization refers to the process of choosing the right pension payout option to receive the maximum benefit for you and your spouse. Here are some pension maximization strategies:

Single Life Annuity Option:

This is the option that is selected automatically by the majority of pension plans, and it will continue to pay you a benefit every month for the remainder of your life. On the other hand, if you die away, your spouse will not be eligible for any benefits.

Joint and Survivor Annuity Option:

This choice will result in a lesser monthly income for you during your lifetime, but it will ensure that your spouse will get some of your pension when you die away. The percentage of your pension that is allocated to your spouse as a benefit is typically between fifty and seventy-five percent.

Pension Bridge:

You may implement this plan by withdrawing a lump amount from your pension and then using that money to buy an annuity. The annuity will provide you with a stream of income until you reach the age at which you become eligible to receive benefits from Social Security. With the help of this technique, you will be able to enjoy a higher regular income throughout the first few years of your retirement.

It is crucial to analyze your financial objectives, your current health situation, and the financial viability of your pension plan when contemplating options to maximize your pension. You might also consider speaking with a financial counselor or an actuary for assistance in making the choice that is most appropriate for your unique circumstances.

Pension Maximization Risks and Trade-offs

The strategy known as "pension maximization" has the goal of extracting the highest possible amount of money from a pension plan on behalf of both you and your spouse. Several distinct approaches are possible for achieving this goal. When deciding whether or not to use this strategy, one must take into consideration the accompanying expenses and risks before making a decision.

One of the key risks that are linked with the use of this strategy is the fact that pension maximization is a strategy that requires a greater level of involvement than just picking the joint and survivor option from the pension plan. For the aim of maximizing one's pension, it is important to obtain life insurance to compensate for the loss of the survivor benefits that would have been provided under the joint and survivor option in the event of death. These benefits would have been granted if the individual had chosen the joint and survivor option. This implies that you are prepared to take the risk that is connected with investing in the life insurance policy to provide the requisite survivor benefits when the time comes. If the insurance does not perform as expected, there is a possibility that the survivor benefits will not be adequate.

Because of your age and the way you are now feeling, there is a chance that the premiums for your life insurance policy will be fairly costly. This will depend on the specifics of your situation. If the cost of the life insurance premiums is too high, then it is likely that using the strategy to maximize one's pension may not result in a financial benefit for the individual.

When using the strategy to get the most out of one's pension, one has to remember to take into account the costs and benefits associated with it. It is necessary for you to renounce the guaranteed survivor benefits that the joint and survivor option provides in exchange for the prospect of a higher income during your lifetime if you choose the joint and survivor option. This is one of the disadvantages of picking the joint and survivor option. This implies that the survivor would not be entitled to the guaranteed benefits that would have been awarded by the joint and survivor option if either you or your spouse were to pass away at an earlier age than was predicted. This is because the joint and survivor option would have granted these benefits if the joint and survivor option had been selected.

The joint and survivor option may provide more protection against inflation than the pension maximizing plan. This is another risk associated with selecting this plan. This is just an additional detriment associated with using this strategy. The cost of living adjustment, more often referred to as COLA is frequently applied to the survivor payments that are granted under the joint and survivor option. There is a possibility that this will prove to be an efficient technique for giving insurance against inflation. Likely, the life insurance policy that is applied in the pension maximizing approach will not supply the level of protection against inflation that is desired.

It is vital to give serious attention to the numerous options available in addition to the dangers that are linked with them before agreeing on the strategy of maximizing the pension benefit. It is not the greatest choice for everyone, but those who want to maximize their income throughout their career may find that it is to their advantage to pursue this course of action. Having said that, this choice is not one that everyone should make.

Pension Maximization Case Studies

In general, pension maximization strategies involve weighing the benefits and drawbacks of various options for taking your pension benefits. You should think about the financial effect on you and your loved ones if you decide to take a lump sum payout or annuitize your benefits.

One example of a potential pension maximization case might involve a retiree who has the option to take a lump sum payment or annuitize their pension benefits. If the retiree is in good health and has a spouse who is also in good health, they might consider taking the lump sum payment and using some of the proceeds to purchase a life insurance policy that would provide income for their spouse in the event of their death. This strategy would allow the retiree to maximize their pension income while also providing a source of income for their spouse in the event of their passing.

On the other hand, if the retiree has a serious health condition or has reason to believe they may not live long enough to fully benefit from their pension payments, they might choose to annuitize their benefits in order to ensure a guaranteed source of income for the remainder of their life.

Ultimately, the decision of whether to maximize your pension benefits through various strategies will depend on your circumstances and financial goals. It may be helpful to work with a financial advisor who can help you assess your options and make informed decisions based on your unique situation.

Real-Life Scenarios Of Pension Maximization Strategies

Implementing a Life Insurance Retirement Plan (LIRP) can be a powerful strategy to maximize your pension in retirement. Here's a scenario illustrating how it could work:

Imagine a couple, diligently contributing to their LIRP while they're still in their working years. Over time, the plan builds up a substantial cash value. Upon retirement, they find themselves with a fully paid-up LIRP, a veritable reservoir of tax-free funds.

At this juncture, they opt for a single-life pension. This option is generally the most lucrative, offering the highest income during retirement as long as both partners are alive. It's a decision made easier knowing the safety net their LIRP provides. If they need additional funds during retirement, they have the flexibility to tap into the cash value of their LIRP, supplementing their income tax-free.

Now, let's consider the death of one partner. If she were to pass away first, he continues to receive the maximum pension income uninterrupted. The single-life pension choice does not reduce his income, which would not be the case with many joint-life pensions.

But what if he were to die first? Here, their foresight in funding a LIRP pays dividends. The death benefit from his fully paid-up LIRP kicks in, replacing what was once a taxable pension with a tax-free income source. This results in more income for her as she navigates her remaining retirement years.

Ultimately, this strategy ensures that, regardless of who passes away first, the surviving partner is left with an optimal, tax-efficient income stream during their retirement.

Visual Representation

Guaranteed income for life for you and your spouse.

Single-life pension	Retire monthly income $3,000	Spouse's monthly income (upon the death of retiree) $0
Combined & survivor pension	Retiree Monthly income $2,400	Spouse's monthly income (upon the death of retiree) $2,400

$600 per month X 20 years = $144,000

Evaluating Your Options Under Four Possible Scenarios

The single-life option plus permanent life insurance. *Please note: there will be an ongoing cost to keep your permanent life insurance policy in force.*	**Your spouse dies first** You receive the higher monthly pension income AND still have a life policy that maximizes your legacy. You can also access the cash value from your policy to supplement your retirement income if needed.	**You die first** While both options can work in this scenario, with the single life option plus permanent life insurance, you leave your spouse the death benefit of the life policy AND you had been receiving the higher monthly pension income as a couple while you were alive.	**You both die together:** The life insurance proceeds can help you pass wealth on to your heirs, generally income tax-free.	**You both live long lives:** You have higher monthly pension income and cane access cash value in the life policy or leave as a legacy.
The Joint & Survivor option	You have the lesser pension income and no cash value from a life policy.	With the joint & Survivor option, you leave your spouse the pension	Relying solely on the join and survivor pension income in this situation	You receive the lower monthly pension income

		income, but the lower monthly value and NO life policy death benefit.	would leave nothing to your beneficiaries.	as a couple with no life cash value to access or death benefit to leave as a legacy.

Permanent life insurance + Single life option = Maximum monthly pension payments & Lifetime protection for your spouse and/or beneficiaries.

Chapter 7

Strategies for Maximizing Retirement Income with Permanent Life Insurance

Permanent life insurance may be utilized in several ways to increase your retirement savings. Some of these strategies include:

Overfunding a policy: This strategy involves contributing more than the minimum required premium into a permanent life insurance policy. By doing so, the policy can accumulate cash value more quickly, which can be used to supplement retirement income in the future.

Using policy loans: The cash value of a permanent life insurance policy may be used as collateral for loans. By taking out policy loans, policyholders can access the cash value of their policy without triggering taxable income. These loans can be paid back over time, or the interest can be paid annually, allowing the policyholder to have more control over their retirement income.

Utilizing cash value withdrawals: Cash value withdrawals allow policyholders to access the cash value of their policy without taking out a loan. These withdrawals are tax-free up to the amount of the policyholder's basis (total premiums paid into the policy) and can provide a source of tax-free retirement income.

Converting the policy to an income stream: Some permanent life insurance policies offer the option to convert the cash value of the policy into a guaranteed income stream, either for a specific period or for the policyholder's lifetime. This can provide a steady source of retirement income that is not subject to market fluctuations.

Leveraging a death benefit: For policyholders who do not need the full death benefit of their permanent life insurance policy, the death benefit can be leveraged to provide a source of retirement income. One option is to sell a part of the policy's death benefit in return for a lump amount of money, a process known as a life settlement or viatical settlement.

These techniques should be carefully reviewed in the context of an individual's entire financial strategy and retirement income objectives since they may not be appropriate for everyone.

Incorporating LIRP/SLIRP Into A Comprehensive Retirement Plan

LIRP/SLIRP (Life Insurance Retirement Plan/Supplemental Life Insurance Retirement Plan) is a strategy that involves using permanent life insurance policies to build cash value that can be used to generate retirement income. Incorporating LIRP/SLIRP into a comprehensive retirement plan involves several steps:

Assessing Retirement Income Needs:

Finding out how much money would be required during retirement is the first thing that has to be done when implementing LIRP/SLIRP into a retirement plan. This necessitates taking into account not just the expenses but also the revenue that will be received during retirement from things like Social Security and pensions.

Choosing the Right Permanent Life Insurance Policy:

The next step is to choose a permanent life insurance policy tailored to the individual based on their risk tolerance and financial goals. Many distinct types of life insurance policies exist, and their names reflect their primary features: whole life, universal, indexed, and variable universal life insurance.

Setting Up the Policy:

After the appropriate insurance has been selected, it is essential to configure it in such a way as to make the most of its potential to serve as a source of income after retirement. This may entail determining the appropriate premium payments, selecting the appropriate death benefit, and making certain that the policy is designed to allow for the greatest possible increase in cash value.

Building Cash Value:

Building up cash value in a permanent life insurance policy is essential if you want to use a LIRP/SLIRP to generate income throughout retirement. This may entail making premium payments that are higher than the minimum needed amount, utilizing profits to acquire extra paid-up insurance, or making use of riders that may expedite the rise of cash value.

Generating Retirement Income:

After the cash value in the insurance has been accumulated to the desired level, it may be tapped into as a source of income during retirement. To do this, you may make use of the policy's withdrawal or loan features or utilize the death benefit to provide a tax-free bequest to heirs.

Monitoring and Adjusting the Plan:

As is the case with any strategy for generating income during retirement, it is essential to keep an eye on the plan throughout time and make any necessary adjustments. In order to guarantee that the individual's plan continues to satisfy their objectives, they may need to reevaluate their requirements for retirement income, make adjustments to their premium payments, or make modifications to the policy structure or investing strategy.

It is necessary to engage in meticulous preparation and pay close attention to the particulars to successfully include LIRP/SLIRP in an all-encompassing retirement plan. However, for those who are ready to put in the work, a LIRP/SLIRP may be an effective method to create retirement income while also giving tax advantages and long-term financial security. For those who are prepared to put in the time and effort, a LIRP/SLIRP might be a reliable source of income throughout their golden years.

Safety Bucket Of Monies In Down Market

The safety bucket is a strategy for financial planning that comprises setting aside a portion of one's portfolio in low-risk assets or cash reserves to aid in safeguarding one's portfolio from market downturns or unanticipated demands. The goal of the safety bucket is to assist in protecting one's portfolio from these market downturns or unforeseen needs. You may have heard the phrase "emergency fund" used to allude to the safety bucket. If the market is volatile, there is concern about the economy, or there are other financial problems, this bucket is meant to act as a safety net.

One of the key advantages of having a safety bucket is that it enables you to avoid making the common mistakes of panic selling or withdrawing too much from your portfolio during times of market volatility. Both of these actions may have a significant impact on your ability to achieve your long-term financial goals. You may also be able to avoid the prospect of being forced to sell assets at a loss in order to pay unplanned expenditures by using this technique, which is something that may be avoided by utilizing this particular strategy.

Your capacity for risk, the goals you want to accomplish with your investments, and the commitments you have made about your money are all elements that will play a role in determining the size of your safety bucket. Having three to six months' worth of liquid assets on hand is recommended by financial experts as a kind of financial contingency planning. This serves as a general rule of thumb for the advice given. It is feasible that the size of the "safety bucket" should be raised for persons who are already retired or who are very near to reaching the age of retirement to provide a better sense of stability and security for these individuals.

To be eligible for placement in the safety bucket, an asset must be minimal in complexity and averse to risk. Some examples of suitable candidates for this category are cash equivalents, high-quality short-term bonds, and savings accounts backed by the FDIC. We will not be concentrating on earning enormous profits; rather, we will work toward safeguarding the original investment and bringing in an amount of interest income that is suitable for our needs.

In general, the safety bucket is a crucial component of a comprehensive retirement plan that may help offer financial security and peace of mind during market downturns or unexpected events. This may aid in giving financial security and peace of mind during market downturns or unexpected occurrences. In addition, the emergency fund may help retirees achieve the financial security and mental calmness that they want throughout their golden years by making it possible for them to contribute to the fund.

Does this look more like your portfolio?

Account alone

Age	S&P 500 Return	Barclays Agg. Bond Index Return	Performance 60% S&P 40% Bond Index	Beginning of Year Balance	Annual Withdrawal	End of Year Balance
65	10.08%	9.75%	9.95%	$1,000,000	($80,000)	$1,011,522
66	1.32%	-2.92%	-0.38%	$1,011,522	($80,000)	$928,019
67	37.58%	18.46%	29.93%	$928,019	($80,000)	$1,101,848
68	22.96%	3.64%	15.23%	$1,101,848	($80,000)	$1,177,496
69	33.36%	9.64%	23.87%	$1,177,496	($80,000)	$1,359,490
70	28.58%	8.70%	20.63%	$1,359,490	($80,000)	$1,543,424
71	21.04%	-0.82%	12.30%	$1,543,424	($80,000)	$1,643,366
72	-9.10%	11.63%	-0.81%	$1,643,366	($80,000)	$1,550,734
73	-11.89%	8.43%	-3.76%	$1,550,734	($80,000)	$1,415,405
74	-22.10%	10.26%	-9.16%	$1,415,405	($80,000)	$1,213,135
75	26.86%	4.10%	17.76%	$1,213,135	($80,000)	$1,334,335
76	10.88%	4.34%	8.26%	$1,334,335	($80,000)	$1,357,993
77	4.91%	2.43%	3.92%	$1,357,993	($80,000)	$1,328,065
78	15.79%	4.33%	11.21%	$1,328,065	($80,000)	$1,387,923
79	5.49%	6.97%	6.08%	$1,387,923	($80,000)	$1,387,471
80	-37.00%	5.24%	-20.10%	$1,387,471	($80,000)	$1,044,617
81	26.46%	5.93%	18.25%	$1,044,617	($80,000)	$1,140,640
82	15.06%	6.54%	11.65%	$1,140,640	($80,000)	$1,184,226
83	2.11%	7.84%	4.40%	$1,184,226	($80,000)	$1,152,834
84	16.00%	4.22%	11.29%	$1,152,834	($80,000)	$1,193,936
85	32.39%	2.02%	18.63%	$1,193,936	($80,000)	$1,321,417

Returns based on blended portfolio—60% stocks, 40% bonds.

Years when portfolio is down.

In this scenario, after 20 years of withdrawals the account is left with $1,321,417.

Based on historical S&P 500 and Barclays Aggregate Bond Index returns for years 1993-2013. The 1993-2013 time period was selected because it represented a time frame with losses distributed throughout the portfolio.

Returns based on a blended portfolio of 60% stocks and 40% bonds.

New York Life Insurance Company (2016).

Let's take a look at this portfolio's potential results after withdrawing income from the cash value in a permanent life insurance policy.

Account and permanent life insurance

Age	S&P 500 Return[1]	Barclays Agg. Bond Index Return[1]	Performance 60% S&P 40% Bond Index	Beginning of Year Balance	Annual Withdrawal	End of Year Balance
65	10.08%	9.75%	9.95%	$1,000,000	($80,000)	$1,011,522
66	1.32%	-2.92%	-0.38%	$1,011,522	($80,000)	$928,019
67	37.58%	18.46%	29.93%	$928,019	$0	$1,205,794
68	22.96%	3.64%	15.23%	$1,205,794	($80,000)	$1,297,275
69	33.36%	9.64%	23.87%	$1,297,275	($80,000)	$1,507,862
70	28.58%	8.70%	20.63%	$1,507,862	($80,000)	$1,722,402
71	21.04%	-0.82%	12.30%	$1,722,402	($80,000)	$1,844,352
72	-9.10%	11.63%	-0.81%	$1,844,352	($80,000)	$1,750,096
73	-11.89%	8.43%	-3.76%	$1,750,096	$0	$1,684,257
74	-22.10%	10.26%	-9.16%	$1,684,257	$0	$1,530,047
75	26.86%	4.10%	17.76%	$1,530,047	$0	$1,801,722
76	10.88%	4.34%	8.26%	$1,801,722	($80,000)	$1,864,005
77	4.91%	2.43%	3.92%	$1,864,005	($80,000)	$1,853,902
78	15.79%	4.33%	11.21%	$1,853,902	($80,000)	$1,972,685
79	5.49%	6.97%	6.08%	$1,972,685	($80,000)	$2,007,799
80	-37.00%	5.24%	-20.10%	$2,007,799	($80,000)	$1,540,234
81	26.46%	5.93%	18.25%	$1,540,234	$0	$1,821,296
82	15.06%	6.54%	11.65%	$1,821,296	($80,000)	$1,944,192
83	2.11%	7.84%	4.40%	$1,944,192	($80,000)	$1,946,253
84	16.00%	4.22%	11.29%	$1,946,253	($80,000)	$2,076,916
85	32.39%	-2.02%	18.63%	$2,076,916	($80,000)	$2,368,862

Years when portfolio is down.

Cash value from life insurance can supplement income in years after the market is down. And, there may be additional cash value and death benefit remaining depending on the size of the policy.

After withdrawing income from another source in the years following a market loss, $2,368,862 is left in the account after 20 years. That's over $1,000,000 more than with the account alone.

[1] Based on historical S&P 500 and Barclays Aggregate Bond Index returns for years 1993-2013. The 1993-2013 time period was selected because it represented a time frame with losses distributed throughout the portfolio.

Returns are based on a blended portfolio of 60% stocks and 40% bonds.

New York Life Insurance Company (2016).

Creating A Customized Strategy That Leverages Permanent Life Insurance For Retirement Income

Creating a customized strategy that leverages permanent life insurance for retirement income involves several steps:

Determine Retirement Income Needs:

To prepare for retirement, one must first determine how much money would be needed for basic living expenses and other financial responsibilities. Calculating estimated living expenditures, which include the price of housing, food, transportation, and healthcare, as well as the costs of any additional anticipated expenses, such as those associated with vacation or hobbies, is one way to accomplish this goal.

Assess The Current Financial Situation:

Next, one should evaluate their current financial situation, taking into account all prospective retirement income sources, including Social Security, pensions, and investment accounts. This might help determine if there is a gap between the retirement income demands and the retirement income sources now available.

Consider Permanent Life Insurance:

After determining the amount of income necessary for retirement as well as the present state of one's finances, one should investigate the possibility of including permanent life insurance as part of the plan for retirement income. When you reach retirement age, you won't owe any taxes when you withdraw the cash value from your permanent life insurance policy, such as whole life, universal life, indexed universal life, or variable universal life policy. Variable universal life, indexed universal life, and other permanent life insurance plans are also available.

Customize The Policy:

After determining the kind of permanent life insurance policy that would bring in the most money after retirement, individuals may next tailor their coverage to match their specific needs. This may entail choosing a certain amount for the death benefit, modifying the structure of the premium payment plan, or adding riders to the policy to give extra benefits.

Coordinate With Other Retirement Income Sources:

Make sure that your requirements for retirement income are satisfied by coordinating the permanent life insurance policy with the other sources of retirement income. For instance, the cash value of a permanent life insurance policy may be used to augment the income received from other sources after retirement, which can be helpful during times of market volatility or other types of financial difficulties.

The benefits of incorporating permanent life insurance into a retirement income strategy include the following:

Tax advantages: Both the growth of the cash value accumulation and any withdrawals made from a permanent life insurance policy are exempt from taxes throughout the policyholder's retirement years.

Flexibility: Permanent life insurance plans provide policyholders with a great deal of leeway in terms of premium payments, the number of death benefits they get, and the degree to which they may customize their coverage, which results in a customized plan for retirement income.

Risk management: In the case of market volatility or other unanticipated financial difficulties, a permanent life insurance policy with cash value accumulation might serve as a safety net.

Legacy planning: It is possible to leave a legacy for loved ones by making use of the death benefit offered by a permanent life insurance policy, or it may be used toward supporting charitable organizations.

Overall, a customized strategy that leverages permanent life insurance can provide a reliable and tax-efficient source of retirement income while also providing protection and flexibility to meet individual needs.

Literally Can Guarantee The Dollar If You Live Too Long Or Die Too Soon

This remark refers to the assurances that are offered by permanent life insurance plans, such as whole life, universal life, indexed universal life, and variable universal life insurance policies.

These plans ensure that the beneficiary will get the full death benefit upon the passing of the policyholder, regardless of the timing of the policyholder's passing. The policyholder's age, health, and preferred level of coverage are often taken into consideration when calculating the death benefit amount. This takes place at the time the policy is issued.

Cash value buildup is another perk that comes with permanent life insurance plans, in addition to the guaranteed reward upon passing away. The insurance firm invests the premiums that are put into the policy, and the cash worth of the policy increases tax-deferred over the course of the policy's term. Policy loans and withdrawals, as well as premium payments, are all viable options for accessing monetary value while the policyholder is still alive and well.

The capacity to guarantee both the increase of the cash value and the distribution of the death benefit is one of the distinctive characteristics of perpetual life insurance plans. Because of this, the policyholder may be certain that the promised benefits will be paid no matter what happens to the market or the economy.

In general, the assurances provided by permanent life insurance policies may be a very useful tool when crafting a plan to safeguard one's retirement income. Individuals may have peace of mind knowing that their retirement income and legacy will be secured regardless of the market circumstances or unanticipated occurrences if they take advantage of these assurances and use them to their advantage.

Building Multiple Streams Of Income In Retirement

Establishing several different avenues via which one might earn a living after retirement is one of the most important steps one can take to ensure financial independence and security throughout their golden years. You may lessen your dependence on any one specific income stream by diversifying your sources of income, giving you more flexibility to pay unforeseen needs, manage risk, and live the retirement lifestyle you prefer.

Here are some ways you can build multiple streams of income in retirement:

1. Social Security: Social Security is a primary source of income for many retirees, providing a guaranteed monthly benefit based on your earnings history. You may begin collecting Social Security benefits as early as the age of 62, but the longer you wait to begin collecting, the bigger your benefit will be when you do start collecting.

2. Pension: If you have a pension plan, it can provide a significant source of retirement income. Your years of service and average income are often used to calculate the amount of the guaranteed monthly benefit that is provided by pension plans. When you are planning your income during retirement, you should make sure that you fully grasp the rules of your pension plan and consider a variety of considerations, including inflation, spousal benefits, and survivor benefits.

3. Retirement Accounts: Retirement accounts such as 401(k)s, IRAs, and annuities are a popular way to save for retirement and provide a steady stream of income in retirement. You can withdraw funds from these accounts in retirement, and the type of account you choose will determine the tax treatment of your withdrawals.

4. Real Estate: Real estate can be a source of passive income in retirement. You can earn rental income from investment properties, or you can sell a primary residence and downsize to a smaller home or a more affordable location and invest the difference.

5. Part-Time Work: Many retirees choose to work part-time in retirement, either to stay active or to supplement their retirement income. Part-time work can provide social interaction, a sense of purpose, and additional income.

6. Permanent Life Insurance: Permanent life insurance plans, such as those offered by whole life insurance companies, may be able to provide a source of income during retirement that is exempt from taxation. By accumulating cash value over time, you can borrow against the policy or receive tax-free withdrawals in retirement.

The benefits of building multiple streams of income in retirement include:

1. Greater financial security: By diversifying your sources of income, you can reduce the impact of market volatility, unexpected expenses, or changes in your circumstances.

2. Flexibility: Multiple streams of income provide greater flexibility to manage your retirement finances and respond to changes in your lifestyle.

3. Increased retirement lifestyle options: With multiple streams of income, you can have the financial resources to pursue your retirement dreams and enjoy your golden years to the fullest.

In conclusion, accumulating numerous sources of income throughout retirement is an important approach for gaining monetary autonomy and flexibility in one's retirement years. You may live the kind of retirement lifestyle you choose while simultaneously lowering your exposure to risk and expanding your range of possibilities if you diversify your sources of income.

Non-Direct Recognition And Income

In terms of income, policy owners can use the cash value of their policy to take policy loans or withdrawals, which are not typically subject to income taxes. This means that the policy owner can use the cash value of the policy as a tax-free source of retirement income.

It's important to note that taking loans or withdrawals from a life insurance policy can reduce the death benefit, and interest may be charged on any outstanding loans. Additionally, policy loans and withdrawals may impact the policy's ability to earn dividends or interest, which could reduce the growth potential of the policy over time.

Overall, non-direct recognition can be an important feature to consider when using permanent life insurance policies to generate retirement income, as it can allow policy owners to access the cash value of their policy without sacrificing the potential for continued growth.

Working With A Financial Advisor To Implement Your Plan

When it comes to putting up a strategy for your retirement income that includes permanent life insurance, consulting with a financial adviser may be an extremely helpful step. Your retirement income plan may benefit from the advice and assistance of a seasoned financial adviser who can provide you with direction and assist you in making choices based on accurate information. Some examples of how a financial advisor could help are provided below.

1. Your lifestyle expenditures, the price of health care, and any other financial commitments may all play a role in determining how much retirement income you will need. Based on these factors, a financial

advisor may help you calculate how much retirement income you'll need.

2. He/She will evaluate your risk tolerance. A financial adviser may assist you in determining your degree of comfort with risk and propose a mix of assets that are in line with your objectives and your level of confidence.

3. Choosing the proper policy for permanent life insurance: A financial adviser can assist you in understanding the many kinds of permanent life insurance policies that are available and can propose a policy that satisfies your particular requirements for income after retirement.

4. Developing a tax-efficient strategy for retirement income: Working with a financial adviser may assist you in developing a tax-efficient strategy for retirement income that takes advantage of the tax advantages offered by permanent life insurance and other retirement vehicles.

5. Monitoring and updating your plan: If you work with a financial adviser, they may assist you in monitoring and revising your retirement income plan as necessary to ensure that it remains in alignment with your objectives and your current financial condition.

Working with a financial adviser may help you construct a retirement income plan that optimizes your income while reducing the amount of risk you take on during your golden years.

Meet Your Advisor At Least Once A Year

To check in on your financial plan and make any required modifications, it's recommended that you see a financial counselor at least once a year. Here are some reasons why meeting with your advisor annually is important:

Review your financial goals: Your financial goals may change from year to year, and it's important to review them regularly with your advisor to ensure your investment strategy aligns with those goals.

Review your portfolio: Your portfolio may need to be rebalanced or adjusted based on market conditions, changes in your financial situation, or changes in your risk tolerance. By examining your portfolio often, your advisor can help you maintain it in line with your goals and tolerance for risk.

Tax planning: Meeting with your advisor can help you plan for potential tax liabilities and find opportunities to reduce your tax burden.

Retirement planning: Review your retirement plan with your adviser as you approach retirement to make sure you are on track to reach your objectives and to make any required modifications.

Life changes: Significant life changes such as marriage, divorce, the birth of a child, or a job change can all impact your financial plan. Regular meetings with your advisor can help ensure your plan is adjusted to accommodate any changes.

In short, meeting with your financial advisor at least once a year is important to ensure your financial plan is on track and to make any necessary adjustments to help you achieve your financial goals.

Chapter 8

SELECTING THE RIGHT PERMANENT LIFE INSURANCE POLICY

Explain How You Chose Your Permanent Life Insurance

Determining your goals and objectives is the first thing you need to do before choosing a permanent life insurance policy that's perfect for you. What do you want to accomplish with the new policy? Are you mainly interested in obtaining security via a death benefit, or do you also want to accumulate capital value and secure an income for retirement?

When you have figured out what you want to accomplish, the next step is to compare the various kinds of permanent life insurance plans, such as whole life, universal life, indexed universal life, and variable universal life insurance. Because every kind of plan comes with its own set of characteristics and advantages, it is essential to examine all of the available alternatives in depth before settling on the one that is the most suitable to meet your requirements.

Working with a knowledgeable and experienced financial adviser who can assist you in navigating the process of obtaining the appropriate permanent life insurance policy for your unique circumstances is something else that should not be overlooked. To guarantee that you are making an educated choice about your insurance coverage, your financial adviser may give you individualized guidance and assist you in analyzing the merits and downsides of each policy alternative.

Factors To Consider

Selecting the right permanent life insurance policy is a critical decision, as it can influence your long-term financial planning and the income approach you employ during retirement. Consider these questions when you shop for permanent life insurance:

Policy Type

Permanent life insurance plans come in a variety of flavors, including whole life, universal life, indexed universal life, and variable universal life. Each kind of insurance has its own perks and disadvantages, so picking the one that fits your needs financially is crucial.

Premiums

Permanent life insurance plans often have premiums that are much more expensive to maintain than term life insurance policies. It is essential to choose a coverage that has a premium payment plan that is not only manageable but also fits comfortably within your financial constraints.

Death Benefit

The amount of money that is paid out by the insurance in the event of the death of the policyholder is referred to as the death benefit. It is essential to choose a policy that provides a death benefit that satisfies not only your requirements but also those of the people who will benefit from your passing.

Cash Value

Cash value is a component of permanent life insurance plans that build up over the course of the policy's duration. This financial value may be put to several uses, including the payment of premiums, the acquisition of a loan, or the withdrawal of money from an account. It is crucial to choose a policy that includes a cash value component that is in line with the objectives you have established for your finances.

Investment Options

Policyholders of some types of permanent life insurance, such as indexed universal life and variable universal life, are granted the ability to invest their premium payments in the stock market. It is critical to choose a plan that enables you to make investments in a manner consistent with your comfort level with risk and the achievement of your monetary objectives.

Riders

A permanent life insurance policy may have extra features, known as riders, that may be added to it to increase the benefits it provides. The expedited death benefit rider, the waiver of premium rider, and the long-term care rider are all examples of common riders. It is essential to choose a plan that provides riders that are tailored to your specific requirements.

When it comes to navigating the complexity of selecting the appropriate permanent life insurance coverage, working with a financial adviser may be of great assistance. They can assist which policy type and features correspond with your financial objectives, and they can also assist you in comparing plans from several insurance firms.

Time Frame, What It Is Used For?

When choosing a policy for permanent life insurance, there are a few different aspects to take into consideration. Some of these aspects include the time period, the objective of the policy, and whether or not it is for legacy planning, retirement planning, or estate planning.

The available amount of time is the first factor that must be taken into account. The goal of purchasing a permanent life insurance policy, such as whole life, indexed universal life, or variable universal life policy, is to provide financial security for the insured individual for their whole life. They are not the same as term life insurance, which only offers protection for a certain period. Therefore, if you want coverage from your life insurance policy that lasts longer than a certain amount of time, selecting a permanent policy is very necessary.

The second step is to consider the policy's ultimate goal. There are many different kinds of permanent life insurance plans, and each one is tailored to meet a specific need. For instance, whole life insurance is a conventional kind of permanent policy. It provides a death benefit in addition to a cash value component, which makes it an attractive choice to prepare for one's legacy. Indexed universal life insurance is a fantastic option for financial preparation for retirement since it was developed to provide adaptable coverage that can be modified as the policyholder's requirements change over time. Those who wish to utilize their life insurance policy as an investment vehicle will find that variable universal life insurance, which includes investing opportunities inside the policy, is an excellent choice.

The last thing you need to think about is whether the insurance is for retirement planning, estate planning, or legacy planning. To ensure that your loved ones get financial support after your death, whole life insurance may be the best option. If you are interested in accumulating capital value and providing a source of income during retirement, you may find that indexed universal life insurance or variable universal life insurance is better suited for your needs.

In conclusion, while choosing a policy for permanent life insurance, you should take into consideration the period, the objective of the policy, and whether it is for legacy planning, retirement planning, or estate planning. You'll be able to choose the best permanent insurance to satisfy your requirements and ambitions if you give these considerations the time and attention they need.

Mutual Life Companies And Features

The policyholders of a mutual life insurance company are the owners of the company, and the business is run for the policyholders' advantage rather than the profit of the investors. They often take the form of organizations that are not-for-profit and have as their primary mission the provision of long-term financial security and stability to their policyholders.

Long-term care insurance, often known as LTCI riders, is one of the benefits that are made available by mutual life insurance companies. Because of this rider, policyholders can tap into their death benefit and use it to pay for long-term care costs if they become unable to conduct daily activities of living such as washing, dressing, or eating. Policyholders may enjoy the peace of mind that comes with knowing they have coverage for any future long-term care bills while also preserving their assets by purchasing an LTCI rider for their policies.

The rider for the waiver of premium is yet another benefit that is made available by mutual life insurance companies. If a policyholder suffers from a complete disability and is unable to work, they will be allowed to cancel their premium payments thanks to this rider. During this time, the policyholder will continue to get coverage from the insurance provider even though the policyholder will not be required to make any more premium payments.

Paid-up additions are another benefit that is made available by firms that provide mutual life insurance. Policyholders are granted the ability to make use of the cash value of their policies to obtain extra insurance coverage without being required to submit to medical underwriting. As a result of this option, policyholders may increase their coverage limits at any time throughout the policy's duration without starting the application procedure again.

In general, mutual life insurance firms provide their policyholders with a variety of features and advantages that may provide them with more financial security as well as better peace of mind. Consider the features and benefits offered by different insurers when selecting a policy for permanent life insurance and go with the one that best fits your long-term financial goals and needs.

Evaluating Different Policy Options And Riders

When evaluating different policy options and riders for permanent life insurance, there are several factors to consider, including:

Death Benefit:

The death benefit is the amount that will be paid to your beneficiaries after your death. You need to give some thought to the amount of protection your loved ones may need if anything happens to you.

Premiums:

You need to look at the premiums of many plans to ensure that you will be able to pay for them over the course of their whole term. While the premiums for certain plans may be cheaper when they are first purchased, they could go up over time. Other policies might have higher premiums, but their rates are more consistent.

Cash Value:

The cash value of permanent life insurance plans grows over time and may be withdrawn tax-free at any moment throughout the policyholder's lifetime. You need to determine the expected cash value of the various policies you have and how you intend to put that cash to use.

Policy Riders:

Permanent life insurance plans may have a variety of riders added to them, including paid-up additions, long-term care insurance, and waivers of premiums. You should analyze these riders to determine whether or not they meet your requirements and objectives.

Company Ratings:

You need to do some research on the ratings of various insurance companies to make sure that they are financially sound and have a solid reputation for providing excellent service to their clients.

Policy Flexibility:

When it comes to altering premiums, death benefits, and cash value, some plans may provide policyholders greater leeway than others. It's crucial that you evaluate the flexibility of different policies and determine whether they suit your needs and goals.

Surrender Charges:

If you terminate your permanent life insurance policy before the specified amount of time, you may be subject to surrender costs. You need to analyze these costs to determine whether or not they are congruent with your long-term objectives.

In general, it is vital to make sure that you buy the proper policy for permanent life insurance by carefully evaluating the various policy choices and riders to make sure that you get the right policy that corresponds with your objectives and goals.

What To Look For In Insurance Companies?

It's important to think about some things, including the following, before selecting an insurance provider:

1. Financial Strength: Check the insurance company's financial strength ratings from reputable rating agencies such as A.M. Best, Standard & Poor's, or Moody's. This will help you determine the insurer's ability to meet its financial obligations.

2. Policy Features: Evaluate the features of the policies offered by the insurance company. Consider factors such as the death benefit, premium payment options, cash value accumulation, and policy guarantees. Choose an insurance company that provides flexible policy features that can be customized to meet your unique needs.

3. Rider Options: Check the availability of policy riders that can enhance your coverage, such as long-term care insurance riders, waiver of premium riders, accidental death riders, etc. Make sure the insurance company offers the riders you need to enhance your policy.

4. Customer Service: Evaluate the level of customer service provided by the insurance company. Check the company's customer service ratings and read customer reviews. Ensure that the insurance company has a good reputation for promptly addressing customer concerns.
5. Premiums: Compare the premium rates of the insurance company with those of other insurers offering similar coverage. Choose an insurance company that offers competitive premium rates that fit your budget.

6. Claims Payment: Evaluate the insurance company's claims payment history. Check the claims payment ratings and read reviews from customers who have made claims. Choose an insurance company that has a good reputation for promptly paying claims.

By considering these factors, you can find an insurance company that meets your needs and offers the policy features, riders, and customer service that you require.

Inside Mutual Life Insurance Companies Is The Safest Place To Put Monies

Mutual life insurance companies are owned by policyholders, not by shareholders or investors seeking a profit. These companies have a long history of financial stability and are regulated by state insurance departments to ensure they maintain sufficient reserves to pay policyholder claims.

When you purchase a policy from a mutual life insurance company, you become a member of the company and are entitled to vote on certain company matters. In addition, policyholders may receive dividends or other distributions from the company's profits.

Compared to stock insurance companies, mutual life insurance companies tend to have a more conservative investment strategy and may prioritize long-term stability over short-term gains. They also aren't as likely to put shareholder profits before policyholders' needs or participate in other dangerous financial practices.

Some mutual life insurance companies offer riders that can enhance the policy's benefits, such as long-term care insurance riders, waiver of premium riders, or paid-up additions riders. These riders can provide additional protection or flexibility for policyholders, depending on their specific needs and goals.

Indeed, mutual life insurance companies are generally considered to be financially stable and safe. This is because mutual companies are owned by their policyholders rather than by shareholders, which means that they are not beholden to outside investors and can focus solely on the interests of their policyholders.

Furthermore, mutual companies are often structured in a way that emphasizes long-term financial stability rather than short-term profit maximization. This can make them more resilient to market fluctuations and economic downturns.

To be sure, no investment or financial instrument is without some degree of risk. While mutual life insurance companies may be considered relatively safe, there is always some degree of risk involved in any investment. Before making any major investment choices, it is wise to do one's homework and talk to a financial advisor.

Overall, mutual life insurance companies offer a reliable and stable option for policyholders seeking to protect their financial future. Finding the right insurance company, policy, and add-ons for your unique situation requires some legwork and comparison shopping.

Chapter 9

INCORPORATING PERMANENT LIFE INSURANCE INTO YOUR FINANCIAL PLAN

"You must gain control over your money or the lack of it will forever control you." – Dave Ramsey

How Permanent Life Insurance Fits Into A Comprehensive Financial Plan

Permanent life insurance may be an essential component of a complete financial plan since it not only pays out a payout upon the policyholder's passing but also serves as a source of income that is exempt from taxes throughout retirement. Permanent life insurance, when used correctly, may give additional advantages in addition to providing security for a person's loved ones in the case of an untimely death.

Utilizing permanent life insurance as an additional source of income during retirement is one method for incorporating permanent life insurance into a financial strategy. Through consistent premium payments made throughout the length of the policy's lifespan, the owner of a permanent life insurance policy has the opportunity to build up cash value in the policy. In the future, this cash value may be withdrawn or used as collateral for a loan against the insurance without incurring any income tax liability. This strategy may provide a way to complement traditional retirement income sources like Social Security and traditional retirement plans like 401(k)s and IRAs while minimizing overall tax liability in retirement. This strategy may be used to augment retirement income in this manner.

Permanent life insurance may also be used as a tool for legacy planning, which is another option to use this kind of coverage in a financial strategy. Policyholders can guarantee that their loved ones are provided with a death benefit that is exempt from taxes by designating beneficiaries for their policies. In addition, perpetual life insurance plans may facilitate the tax-wise transmission of wealth to succeeding generations of the insured's family.

When determining the role that permanent life insurance plays in an individual's overall financial strategy, it is essential to take into account a variety of factors, including the potential for cash value accumulation within the policy, the cost of insurance, the stability of the insurance provider's finances, as well as the person's unique financial objectives and requirements. It is highly encouraged to consult with a financial expert who can assist in the evaluation of the numerous insurance possibilities and identify which option is the best match for the individual's specific set of circumstances.

The Customized Strategy That Leverages Permanent Life Insurance For Both Standard Deductions And Retirement Income

A customized strategy that leverages permanent life insurance for both standard deductions and retirement income involves a comprehensive financial planning approach that takes into account a person's specific financial goals, tax situation, risk tolerance, and time horizon. Below are some steps to create a strategy

Determine Your Financial Goals:

It is essential to establish your long-term financial objectives before including permanent life insurance in your strategy for financial security. This encompasses both short-term objectives, such as eliminating debt, and long-term objectives, such as retiring comfortably or leaving behind an enduring legacy.

Assess Your Risk Tolerance:

Before choosing a policy for permanent life insurance, it is crucial to have an accurate assessment of your comfort level with risk. This requires you to evaluate your capacity to deal with changes in the interest rate environment or the stock market.

Determine Your Time Horizon:

The amount of time you have before you use the money that your permanent life insurance policy provides is referred to as your time horizon. When thinking about the several investing possibilities available under the policy, this is a crucial consideration.

Work With A Financial Advisor:

A financial adviser may assist you in evaluating your current financial condition, determining your long-term financial objectives, and developing a bespoke plan that may include purchasing permanent life insurance.

Consider Tax Benefits:

Permanent life insurance plans provide their holders with several tax advantages, including tax-free development of cash value as well as tax-free cash value withdrawals over the policy's lifetime. When formulating a plan, it is essential to take into account the effects that your investments will have on your taxes.

Choose The Right Policy:

Permanent life insurance comes in several different flavors, the most prevalent of which are whole life, universal life, and variable life. Each kind of coverage comes with its own unique set of advantages and potential drawbacks. It is essential to choose the appropriate insurance that corresponds to your individual financial objectives and level of comfort with risk.

Add Riders:

Many different riders may be added to permanent life insurance plans. Some examples of these riders are long-term care insurance riders and premium waiver riders. These riders can provide your policy extra advantages. To get better coverage, you may want to think about adding riders to your insurance.

By incorporating permanent life insurance into your financial plan, you can create a customized strategy that leverages the tax benefits and investment options of a permanent life insurance policy to help meet your financial goals, both for standard deductions and retirement income.

Work With A Financial Advisor To Implement Your Plan.

When implementing an all-encompassing financial strategy that includes permanent life insurance, working with a financial adviser may be a very useful tool. Here are some steps to consider when working with a financial advisor:

1. Identify your goals: Before meeting with a financial advisor, you should identify your financial goals, such as retirement income, legacy planning, or long-term care planning. This will help your advisor to tailor a plan that fits your specific needs.

2. Choose a qualified financial advisor: Look for a financial advisor who has experience working with permanent life insurance and is knowledgeable about the different policy options and riders available.

3. Discuss your financial situation: During your initial meeting, discuss your financial situation with your advisor, including your income, assets, debts, and expenses. This information will help your advisor to create a personalized plan that meets your needs.

4. Review policy options: Your financial adviser should walk you through the many policy alternatives available to you, such as whole life, universal life, and indexed universal life insurance, and explain the advantages and disadvantages associated with each choice.

5. Evaluate riders: Depending on your needs, your advisor may recommend adding riders to your policy, such as long-term care insurance or a waiver of premium rider. Be sure to discuss the cost and benefits of each rider with your advisor.

6. Monitor your plan: Once your plan is in place, your advisor should monitor your policy and adjust it as needed to ensure it continues to meet your goals and objectives.

In general, engaging with a financial adviser may assist you in the process of developing a tailor-made plan that makes use of permanent life insurance for both normal deductions and income after retirement. By carefully assessing your needs and working with a qualified advisor, you can create a plan that provides financial security for you and your family.

Incorporating Roth IRAs in Your Retirement Strategy

Roth Individual Retirement Accounts and Their Importance in a Retirement Strategy Discussion A Roth IRA is an important part of any retirement strategy. In contrast to standard IRAs, Roth IRA contributions are made after taxes and may be withdrawn tax-free in retirement. The Roth IRA is not just a great way to save for retirement, but also a potent instrument for tax planning and asset preservation because of this. It may provide a steady and tax-free income stream in retirement, much like permanent life insurance.

Interaction Between Roth IRAs and Permanent Life Insurance

Both Roth IRAs and permanent life insurance policies have their own advantages, but they may work together to provide a more well-rounded retirement strategy. A perpetual life insurance policy, for instance, may either pay out a death benefit to the policyholder's beneficiaries or grow monetary value over time (Johnson, 2023) or both. In addition to providing financial security in retirement, the cash value component may be borrowed against if required. Both may help you save money on taxes and provide security for your loved ones when you're gone, making them essential components of any retirement strategy.

Financial Planning Advice On Making The Most Of Your Roth IRA

Planning ahead is essential for getting the most out of Roth IRAs. First, start saving as soon as possible and put away as much as you can each month to maximize the benefits of compound interest. Second, if your salary puts you beyond the limit for a Roth IRA, you may want to consider backdoor or super backdoor options. Finally, it's important to note that early withdrawal of profits from a Roth IRA may be subject to taxes and penalties, despite the fact that withdrawals themselves are tax-free. Therefore, to get the most out of your Roth IRA, you should not touch it until retirement.

When incorporating these resources into your financial strategy, it is essential to consult with a financial counselor. You may rely on their knowledge to create a strategy that is unique to your situation.

Conclusion

"More important than the how we achieve financial freedom, is the why. Find your reasons why you want to be free and wealthy." — Robert Kiyosaki, businessman

Here is a recap of the benefits of using permanent life insurance for meeting standard deductions and building retirement income:

1. Tax Benefits: Permanent life insurance offers tax benefits such as tax-deferred growth of cash value, tax-free withdrawals and loans, and tax-free death benefit payments to beneficiaries.

2. Guaranteed Income: Permanent life insurance policies offer a guaranteed death benefit and may also provide a guaranteed stream of income during retirement through the use of riders.

3. Asset Protection: The cash value of permanent life insurance policies is typically protected from creditors and can be used to provide a source of funds for emergencies or unexpected expenses.

4. Estate Planning: Permanent life insurance can be used as an estate planning tool to provide funds for estate taxes or to leave a legacy to heirs.

5. Flexibility: Permanent life insurance policies offer flexibility in terms of premiums, death benefits, and investment options, which can be adjusted as needed over time to meet changing needs.

Consultation with a financial planner may help you decide whether permanent life insurance is the right way to secure your financial future.

In conclusion, it's possible to reap several benefits by including permanent life insurance in your retirement plan, including tax-free growth, tax-free withdrawals, and a death benefit that may help protect your loved ones financially in the case of your untimely demise. You may withdraw the cash value of a permanent life insurance policy tax-free once you reach retirement age. This can help you make the most of your retirement income and ensure that you can maintain the style of living you wish throughout your golden years.

It is crucial to engage with a financial adviser who can help you pick the correct policy and build a plan that matches your financial objectives and circumstances to make the most of the retirement income you get from permanent life insurance. This will allow you to maximize the amount of money you receive from this kind of insurance. They can help you understand the risks and trade-offs involved in purchasing permanent life insurance and guide you through the process.

In addition, it is essential to frequently assess and adapt your retirement plan as the conditions of your life change. This should be done whenever big life events take place, such as getting married, having a kid, or experiencing a large shift in either income or spending. You may guarantee that you are on pace to reach your financial objectives and optimize your retirement income via the use of permanent life insurance by working with a financial adviser, routinely evaluating and changing your retirement plan, and constantly reviewing and amending your retirement plan.

References

Bankrate. (n.d.). Roth IRA vs. Roth 401(k): How they differ. https://www.bankrate.com/retirement/roth-ira-vs-roth-401k-how-they-differ/

Bennett, S. (2023) Knowledge Is Everything: Roosevelt Net Worth. https://caknowledge.com/franklin-roosevelt-net-worth/

Busse, P. (n.d.). Retirement Planning with Permanent Life Insurance. https://www.peterbusse.com/files/5197/13544.pdf

Chen, J. (2023). The Backdoor Roth IRA: How High Earners Can Take Advantage. Investopedia.

Fidelity. (2023). Roth IRA Contribution Limits for 2023. https://www.fidelity.com

Forbes. (2023). Roth IRA Contribution Limits for 2023. https://www.forbes.com

Guardian Life. (n.d.). Permanent Life Insurance. https://www.guardianlife.com/life-insurance/permanent

Gordon, M. (2013). ALM: Think Advisor. Bernanke's largest investment holdings are two annuities. https://www.thinkadvisor.com/2013/08/28/bernankes-largest-investment-holdings-are-two-annuities/

Guardian Life. (n.d.). Whole Life Insurance for Retirement. https://www.guardianlife.com/life-insurance/whole-life/retirement

Haye P. (2015). Personal Work Sheet Tax efficiency Analysis: Taxed currently, taxed later, taxed later.

IRS. (2023). Retirement Topics - IRA Contribution Limits. IRS.gov.

IRS. (2023). Roth IRA Contribution Limits for 2023. https://www.irs.gov

Insuranceopedia. (n.d.). Direct recognition life insurance vs. non-direct: Which is better? Insuranceopedia. https://www.insuranceopedia.com/direct-recognition-life-insurance-vs-non-direct-which-is-b

Investopedia. (2021, March 22). Roth 401(k) vs. Roth IRA: Which is Better for You? https://www.investopedia.com/articles/personal-finance/063015/roth-401k-vs-roth-ira-one-better.asp

Investopedia. (2021, February 2). Tax Code, Rules, and Regulations: What You Need to Know. https://www.investopedia.com/articles/tax/09/tax-codes-rules-regulations.asp

Investopedia. (2021). Roth 401(k) Contribution Limits for 2023. https://www.investopedia.com

Investopedia. (2018, October 2). Life Insurance vs. IRA Retirement Saving: What You Need to Know. https://www.investopedia.com/articles/personal-finance/100215/life-insurance-vs-ira-retirement-saving.asp

Investopedia. (2019, September 25). How Permanent Life Insurance Can Cut Your Taxes. https://www.investopedia.com/articles/pf/07/permanent_life_insurance_taxes.asp

Johnson, M. (2023). The synergistic effects of Roth IRAs and permanent life insurance in retirement planning. Journal of Financial Planning, 36(2), 50-60.

MassMutual. (n.d.). Insurance as a retirement supplement. MassMutual. https://blog.massmutual.com/post/insurance-retirement-supplement

McBride, W. (2023). The Power of Compound Interest: Why You Should Invest in a Roth IRA Now. Forbes.

New York Life Insurance Company (2016). The Company You Keep. www.newyorklife.com

New York Life. (n.d.). Term or Permanent Life Insurance: Which is Right for You? https://www.newyorklife.com/articles/term-or-permanent-life-insurance

Nationwide. (n.d.). Advantages of Permanent Life Insurance. https://www.nationwide.com/lc/resources/investing-and-retirement/articles/advantages-of-permanent-life-insurance

O'Donnell, C. (2014) The Rockefellers: The Legacy Of History's Richest Man. Forbes.

Olinga, L. (2022). The Street Investing: Wells Fargo, Citi and JPMorgan Chase Take the Stage. https://www.thestreet.com/investing/big-u-s-banks-to-tell-all-about-the-economy

Osman, J. (2019). Forbes: Amid GE Pension Crisis, Welch & Immelt Should Pay Back Their $600 Million Golden Handshake: https://www.forbes.com/sites/jimosman/2019/11/19/ge-jack-welch-jeff-immelt-pension-crisis-payback/?sh=91ce41c787cd

Progressive. (n.d.). Types of Life Insurance. https://www.progressive.com/answers/life-insurance-types/

SmartAsset. (n.d.). How to use life insurance to pay for retirement. SmartAsset. https://smartasset.com/life-insurance/how-to-use-life-insurance-to-pay-for-retirement

The Co-operators. (n.d.). Types of Life Insurance. https://www.cooperators.ca/en/resource-centre/protect-what-matters/types-of-life-insurance

Truth Concepts. (2016, May 26). Direct recognition vs. non-direct recognition. Truth Concepts. https://truthconcepts.com/direct-recognition-vs-non-direct-recognition-3/

Yellen, P. (2010). Bank On yourself: Famous people who use the bank on yourself method: https://www.bankonyourself.com/famous-people-who-use-the-bank-on-yourself-method.html

Made in the USA
Monee, IL
05 November 2026

67381716R00071